SWIMMING

JOHN VERRIER

THE CROWOOD PRESS

First published in 1985 by
THE CROWOOD PRESS
Crowood House, Ramsbury
Marlborough, Wiltshire SN8 2HE

Reprinted 1986, 1988
Paperback edition 1988
Reprinted 1989

British Library Cataloguing in Publication Data

   Verrier, John
     Swimming.— (Crowood sports books)
     1. Swimming
     I. Title
     797.2'1   GV837
     ISBN 0 946284 02 4 (HB)
            1 85223 031 2 (PB)

Dedicated to Bert Kinnear

Acknowledgements

Cover photograph of Adrian Moorhouse courtesy All-Sport Photographic
Ltd

The author extends his thanks to Joe Dixon for the underwater
photographs and Figs 36, 77, 89, 90, 92, 103, 104, 106, 107 and 110; to
Laurel Keeley for the line illustrations; and to Maureen O'Brien for
the typing.

Photographs not mentioned above by the author

Series Adviser David Bunker, Lecturer, University of Loughborough

Typeset by Inforum Typesetting, Portsmouth
Printed in Great Britain by Redwood Burn Ltd, Trowbridge

Contents

John Verrier is currently the ASA's Education Officer. During a long and distinguished association with swimming in this country, he has held many coaching and administrative posts, including coach to a variety of British teams and international swimmers, team manager at the 1972 Olympics and Director of Swimming Training for the ASA. He was also founder President of the British Swimming Coaches Association.

John Verrier has, over the past two decades, been instrumental in educating many of the country's leading coaches and thousands of swimming teachers in the fundamental principles of teaching and coaching.

This very authoritative publication provides swimmers, teachers, coaches and parents with an in-depth yet easy to read book covering the whole spectrum of the sport of swimming.

David R. Bance
Secretary, British Swimming Coaches
Association

I have known and had the pleasure of working with John Verrier for many years. John has always been very willing to disseminate his considerable knowledge of swimming via the tutoring of recognised teaching and coaching awards in addition to his many practical coaching sessions.

The publication of this excellent and long overdue book will allow his knowledge and understanding of the teaching and coaching of swimming from grass roots to Olympic standard to be shared by a very much wider audience. Teachers, coaches, swimmers and administrators at all levels will find within this book the necessary guidance to understand fully the basic principles of swimming.

I believe this book will make a significant contribution to the advancement of swimming in Great Britain.

Maurice E. Sly, Commonwealth and
Olympic Coach

1 The Mechanics of Swimming

Approximately two-thirds of the earth's surface is covered with water. Of that volume of water well over 90 per cent is salty, which leaves a remainder of a few per cent of fresh water. Much of the fresh water is locked in the ice caps, which means remarkably little fresh water of the appropriate temperature is available for swimming.

Swimming itself has widely differing meanings. At one end of the scale is the person who goes daily into the sea during an annual holiday and, at the other, the supreme athletes who train for up to twenty-five hours weekly in hard sessions all the year round. Sadly, in Britain there are areas where swimming is not possible due to lack of safe facilities and, sadder still, are the older members of our population who never had opportunity to learn when young, leaving much work to be done with adult beginners. Saddest of all in one way are the handicapped people, although a national upsurge of provision for the less fortunate is more than evident, and some local authorities must be applauded for their efforts.

Whether you swim in salt or fresh water, certain principles remain the same. In water, the average human body becomes virtually weightless. Salt water gives more support than fresh, due to the denser solution made by chemicals dissolved in the water. Cold water is denser than warm water, so the greatest support would be found in cold, salty water, but only polar bears are likely to enjoy it. Very warm water is capable of absorbing greater quantities of chemicals, but the mixture is painful to the eyes, as visitors to the Dead Sea or the Gulf of Mexico will know, even though great support to a floater is given. Most of us will accept the treated fresh water of the local pool, with its temperature of around 80°F or 27°C.

BODY COMPOSITION
(Figs 1 to 7)

The human body is composed of many kinds of tissue, but the most important from the point of view of flotation are the quantities of bone, muscle and fat. In a stew, the bone and the meat, which is the muscle of the animal being cooked, sink to the bottom of the pot, while the fat accumulates on the surface. Similarly, when a person gets into the swimming pool, the bone and muscle will tend to sink, while the fat will float. The combination of the proportions of these three tissues will decide whether or not an individual will float high or low in the water, and whether the person will be one of the unlucky few who are classified as 'sinkers', who have no part of their body above the water at all. It must be understood that this is not common, as most people float reasonably comfortably.

It is not only the proportions of bone, muscle and fat that are to be considered, but their distribution as a deciding factor on the angle at which individual people float. Should all the passengers in a boat crowd towards its stern, then the stern will sink and the bow rise.

A man with heavily boned and muscled legs will float at a great angle, even vertically, and

1

The Mechanics of Swimming

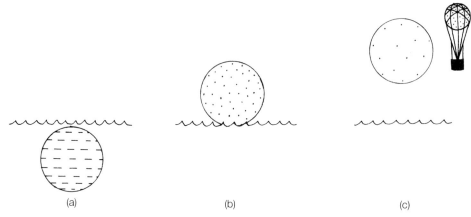

Fig 1   Buoyancy; (a) A bladder full of water
behaves like the water surrounding; (b)
a bladder full of air floats very high; (c) a
bladder full of hydrogen floats in air.

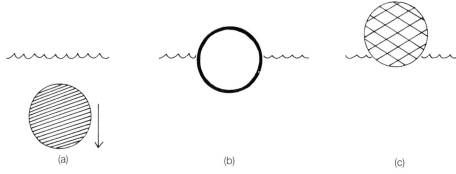

Fig 2   (a) A solid iron ball sinks; (b) a hollow
iron ball floats; (c) a solid wooden ball
floats.

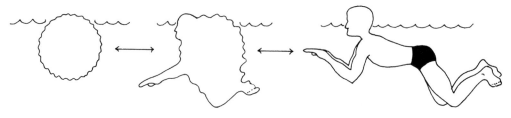

Fig 3   A mixture of air, muscle, fat and bone
just floats, and can be reshaped into a
swimmer.

there are individuals whose floating position is upright about eighteen inches below the surface. These rare people are still able to learn to swim, as will be explained later.

Weight and Mass

Earlier, it was said that the human body is virtually weightless in water, and in view of the explanations above concerning individual floating positions, some short statement of the difference between *weight* and *mass* must be made. A person's weight is a variable, depending on where he or she happens to be. An astronaut is weightless, in the sense that a swimmer is weightless. A more common example is the sensation felt when a lift starts or stops, with the feeling of either an increase or decrease in weight to the passenger.

Should the astronaut or the swimmer collide with something, it will still be a painful experience due to the mass of that person, even though he might be weightless.

Flotation *(Figs 8 to 17)*

An important consideration in a person's flotation is the capacity of the lungs, and whether they are filled or not. For the individual who is heavily muscled and who has heavy bones, but who has little fat, the flotation given by air in the lungs is critical, and the swimming

Fig 4   Extra buoyancy, as with air in the lungs, creates an angled floating position.

Fig 5   Poor loading, as by pushing the head down, lifts the other end.

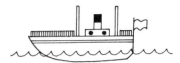

Fig 6   Even loading creates a stable flat floating position.

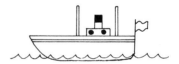

Fig 7   Light loading creates a high, comfortable floating position.

Fig 8   For balance, the weight must be directly above the centre of gravity.

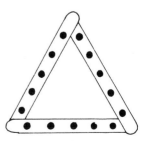

Fig 9   A triangle made from Meccano has its centre of gravity outside itself when placed flat on a table, as also seen in starts and turns.

styles adopted will be modified to meet this. For those born with good flotation, the problems are much decreased.

The *centre of buoyancy*, or *centre of flotation* is that point where all the forces involved in flotation appear to act.

The *centre of gravity* is that point where all the weight of a body, whether human or otherwise, appears to act. An object falls over when its centre of gravity falls outside its body, a concept important in diving.

In the human body, the centre of gravity is usually close to the navel, and is closer to the front of the body than the back. The position of the centre of buoyancy relative to the centre of gravity will decide the natural floating position of the individual concerned.

It cannot be stressed too much that for learners, a basic instruction should always be to keep the shoulders and arms under the water, which places as much of the body as possible in the water to give maximum flotation. This applies to pushing off from the side, when beginners, or nervous swimmers, often lift their arms, and equally often their heads, to keep their faces out of the water. The weight of the arms, head and shoulders, causes the learner to sink, so it is common to see beginners push from the side and sink at once, so that they stop, stand up, then start again, often to repeat the process, when a calm, simple instruction to keep arms and shoulders under the surface helps cure the problem.

RESISTANCE

A skilled swimmer has his body flat, when viewed from the side, as this reduces resistance. To experience just how powerful the resistance of water can be, it is only necessary to be in water of chest depth and to try to walk quickly or to run. Learners, anxious perhaps to keep one or both feet near the floor of the

pool, attempt to swim in angled positions. Some elderly people, due either to their personal floating position, or because they lack strength, also swim in an angled position, which creates resistance.

However, there is the fact that resistance is largely a problem deriving from speed. The faster an object moves through a fluid, the greater the resistance. Learners and recreational swimmers are not interested in speed and so can swim in a position which would be unacceptable for an expert swimmer, who is seeking maximum speed and minimum resistance. For the expert swimmer, resistance is a powerful opposition, because it obeys an inverse square law. Should the expert double his swimming speed, he will have quadrupled the resistance. If his speed is increased four times, the resistance will have increased sixteen times. This is why some teachers and coaches of swimming are heard to say that the only two factors worth talking about are resistance and propulsion.

When an object moves through a fluid, regardless of its shape, it will create resistance. A canoe is shaped to give speed, with low resistance, while a canal barge is built to carry heavy loads at low speeds, so minimum streamlining is wanted, because the barge moves too slowly to build up resistance.

For the skilled, racing swimmer, achieving a streamlined shape is not the end of the problem, as his surface creates friction and tends to drag a 'skin' of water along. Some time ago, swimmers wore swimsuits of woollen material, which created surface friction, but nowadays man-made materials are available which give little resistance.

Swimwear

On the subject of swimwear, there are some important factors for swimmers who race and who have to train for long hours. The suit

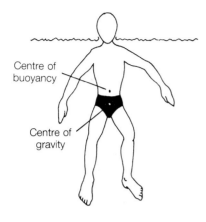

Centre of
buoyancy

Centre of
gravity

Fig 11   With the centres of buoyancy and
gravity closer together it is easier for
the body to float in a streamlined
swimming position.

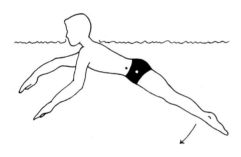

Fig 12   Burying the head in the water causes
the hips to rise and consequently
causes the feet to come out of the
water. Head position in all swimming
strokes has to be adjusted to place
the individual in the best swimming
position attainable.

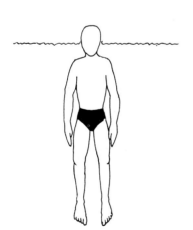

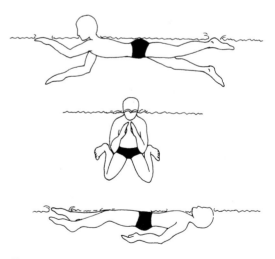

Fig 10   The swimmer has a wide gap between
his centres of gravity and buoyancy
and he will sink until his centre of
gravity is directly below his centre of
buoyancy.

Fig 13   In all these positions, the swimmer is
keeping as much of the body as
possible immersed to gain maximum
flotation.

5

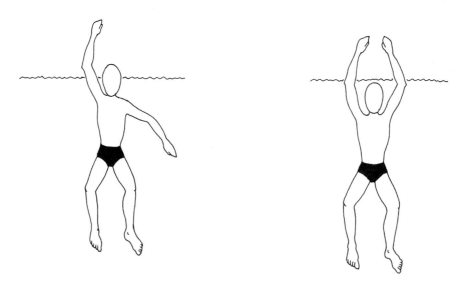

Fig 14   Lifting an arm causes the body to sink;
          lifting both arms causes the body to
          submerge.

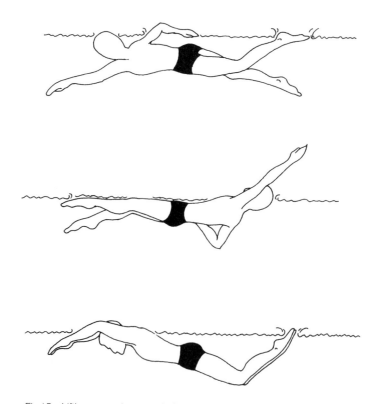

Fig 15   Lifting an arm happens in the normal
          course of swimming frontcrawl,
          backcrawl and butterfly.

Fig 16   A learner pushes off with the head,
shoulders and arms out of the water.
Gravity will pull them down and it is
highly probable the face will go under.
Beginners should always start by
submerging the shoulders.

Fig 17   This learner has discovered that the
hips have to be close to the surface for
easy swimming – and that goes for the
head as well.

should be close fitting, to avoid trapping air bubbles which influence the floating position and its streamlining. For girls there is need for a high necked suit to ensure that there is no drogue effect. A low cut suit is attractive and ideal for the beach holiday, but a serious swimmer would find a drogue literally a drag. Two-piece suits are also for fun wear, because the tightness of the strap impedes breathing.

When buying a swimsuit, girls should look carefully at the kind of stitching inside the shoulder straps, where cheaper suits sometimes have hard thread. In a long training session, with the shoulders rotating continuously, such stitching can cause discomfort, or damage the skin with 'shoulder burns'.

One last word to competitive swimmers. Always check your bag before you leave home and always carry an extra suit. You might need several to cater for your competition needs and there have been some un-happy swimmers rushing about at the last minute to borrow a suit, before competing in an ill-fitting one, which is not likely to put him or her in the best frame of mind.

Having reduced friction by careful choice of swimwear, competitors at the highest levels are known to shave the hairs from the body. Men remove the hairs from their legs, their chests and even their heads, and women are to be seen smoothing their arms and legs with pumice stone. Those who have 'shaved down' say that the body feels electric in the water, but it is debatable as to whether any worthwhile gain over resistance is made, or whether the whole thing is a mental process. Shaving the head is rather an extreme step, but many competitors wear a swimming cap or hat which gives considerable smoothing.

An object moving through a fluid leaves a swirling eddy behind it. In a fast moving river, there is a reversal, because the water is moving and a boulder is still, but behind the boulder the swirling, bubbling eddy can be seen and often heard. These eddies are forms of resistance and swimmers create them when moving through water. Who has not sat in a boat and trailed fingers in the water? A parallel effect is created by moving the body along, by using the arms and by kicking the legs. Skilled swimmers reduce their eddies as much as possible by using highly developed and practised techniques.

Summary

To sum up these comments on resistance, it can be said that resistance is a problem for all swimmers, but particularly so for beginners and for those who for one reason or another, such as poor flotation, or stiff shoulders and ankles, cannot achieve a good swimming position or use their limbs freely. In fact, much of learning to swim is simply the elimination of resistance, with consequent savings in energy needs, regardless of which of the strokes is employed.

PROPULSION

'Resistance and propulsion are the only two factors worth talking about in swimming.' Propulsion is obtained from the arms and from the legs, which can be described as levers, and from the hands and feet, which are used as paddles, or as flippers. All animal movement, which includes human movement, depends on having a skeleton, to give rigidity, with hinges called joints, which permit movement as muscles open and close the joints. Movement is created by shortening a lever, in bending it and then straightening it. An immediate example is the action of walking upstairs, where the alternate bending and straightening of the legs takes the person up. The same action occurs in walking downstairs

and in walking along a level road.

Flexion and Extension

Similar actions can be seen in climbing a rope, where first one arm is straight and the other bent, and the climber moves up the rope by alternately bending and straightening the arms. A more formal term is flexion (bending of a joint) and extension (straightening of a joint). The largest joint in the human body is the hip, which is powerfully used in weightlifting, and in swimming it is powerfully used in butterfly and also in starts and turns. Less obviously, the hip is used when walking, running and also in swimming all strokes, when the large muscles operating around the massive hip joint can be used to great advantage. A swimmer who does not learn this, or is not taught it, is at a disadvantage in trying to get propulsion from the weaker muscles which function at the knee.

A person who is unfortunate enough to have a fractured limb in plaster, finds it impossible to flex and to extend the joints involved. Movement becomes slow and difficult, with inflexible levers. Slow movement is often used by completely flexible people when they are merely sauntering along. No speed is needed, so there is little need for large flexion at the knee. In the water an exact parallel happens when those swimmers who have no interest in speed, but only in a little gentle exercise and enjoyment, are to be seen swimming with long arms and legs, or 'long levers'. There is no need for a lot of bending and straightening, and it should be recalled that it is not necessary because the slow swim they use does not call for a lot of exertion to overcome resistance.

However, should the slow walker have to run to catch a bus, he will immediately flex the knees more in order to be able to extend them strongly to gain speed. In swimming, slow pace often derives from little flexion of the elbow, but those who swim fast bend their arms up to 90 degrees in order to derive maximum propulsion. It is an amusing exercise for a teacher to set a class of children, or for an individual to attempt, to try swimming with perfectly straight arms and legs. It is not possible, but some excited children will claim success although observation will show that there is flexion and extension, however slight, at the elbow, knee, wrist or ankle. This flexion allows subsequent extension which results in propulsion.

Newton's Law *(Fig 18)*

Many children still learn Sir Isaac Newton's law that for every action there is an equal and opposite reaction. Everyday examples are plentiful, such as the recoil of a gun when its missile flies in the opposite direction. A person trying to push a car stranded on a patch of ice is likely to find that his effort sends him backwards as well.

In swimming, Newton's third law of equal action and reaction is demonstrated as the hand reaches forward and shapes to press on the water and the body reacts by moving in the opposite direction. The shaping and pressing of the hands and of the feet, is called 'fixing', which is misleading because perfect fixing is impossible, even for the finest of swimmers. A certain amount of slip will occur and those who have tried running on sand or on snow covered surfaces will know the feeling.

Swimming teachers are often heard telling their classes 'push towards your feet'. This elementary instruction produces the needed action and the correct reaction, although the structure of the body, with the arms shoulder width apart, makes it impossible to push the hands in a straight line towards the feet directly. As the hands deviate from a straight line,

Newton's third law of action and reaction apply so that the feet react towards the hands, or hand. A foot reaction to the movement of the arms is seen in all swimmers, usually in a marked fashion if the swimmer is a learner.

Having said that the hands push towards the feet, which react in turn towards the hands, it should be said that hips react away from the hands at the same time, which gives rise to the snake-like progress of some beginners. The reaction of feet and hips is an important point to which reference will be made later.

Propulsion, for some swimmers therefore, is gained by application of Newton's third law, applied to the arms and legs as levers, with the feet and hands as paddles or flippers. Mainly beginners and recreational swimmers will utilise Newtonian laws in gaining propulsion. Before continuing with rather more sophisticated methods of gaining propulsion, it should be noted that there is nothing wrong in swimming by using what could be called old fashioned strokes and techniques, involving long arms, or levers, with little elbow flexion. If it suits the individual swimmer, physically and mentally, it can only be good, although competitive swimmers would have to adapt the technique to obtain success.

The Bernoulli Principle *(Fig 19)*

In 1844, the Royal Navy could not decide on the choice between paddle steamers or propeller driven steamers. Two ships of identical hulls and with identical steam engines were built, but HMS *Rattler* was driven by a propeller and HMS *Alecto* had paddles. The two ships were joined stern to stern for a tug of war trial. At the given signal, both ships went full ahead and in the event, HMS *Rattler's* propeller proved the better, for HMS *Alecto* was towed backwards.

(a)

(b)

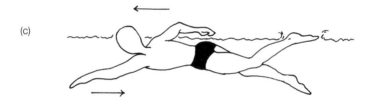

(c)

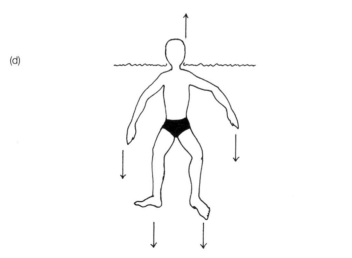

(d)

Fig 18   Newton's law of action and reaction shown (a) in paddling; (b) in breaststroke; (c) in frontcrawl; (d) in sculling.

A propeller creates thrust or lift, depending on which way it is facing. Lift happens when fluid flows over an arranged shape, an aeroplane wing for example, so that low pressure occurs over the wing and the high pressure underneath lifts the wing into the air. Many people possess a hatchback car, with its squarish rear end. At one time cars did not need a screen wiper at their rear, but hatchbacks create high pressure in front and low pressure at their rear, so that road dirt and rain are sucked onto the rear window. A wiper to deal with it becomes a safety feature.

A wing, then, creates lift and a propeller is a wing engineered into a twisted form, so that when it is rotated at the appropriate speed, the lift is delivered as thrust. It must be at the appropriate speed, because the wing of the aeroplane will not lift into the air until flying speed is reached after accelerating along the runway. The blades of a helicopter rotating slowly will not lift the weight into the air, but as they speed up, lift is created by air flowing over the blades and flight ensues.

This method of producing lift, or thrust, is referred to as the Bernoulli principle, after the man who stated it. A review of books, drawings and photographs published before it was realised that Bernoulli principles are employed by outstanding swimmers, reveals that it is quite natural and that in all probability talented swimmers down the generations have always used them.

Human hands and feet can be stiff to form paddles for Newtonian mechanics of action and reaction, but they are also flexible and are placed on arms and legs which twist, or rotate, so that they are capable of acting as propellers. Most people, including children, enjoy finding this for themselves when visiting the pool. Standing still, with shoulders submerged, try sculling with a hand a few inches below the surface of the water. Sculling is an inward push of the hand, thumb up, with the hand pitched, or angled, at roughly 45 degrees, followed by an outward push, with the little finger up. The movement is continuous and it is successful when the performer sees a vortex appear like the one which is seen as a bath empties. Weak or unskilled sculling will produce a small vortex, but strong, practised sculling generates a large vortex, which can be deepened by slowly lowering the sculling hand in the water. Good sculling is essential and all learners should be encouraged to practise it and to feel and learn the sensation it produces in the hand.

Pitch

The word 'pitch' has been used already to describe the angle at which the hand, or the feet, press on the water. As the hands press through their complete action, there is a change of pitch which creates lift, or thrust by a difference in pressure. In creating the vortex

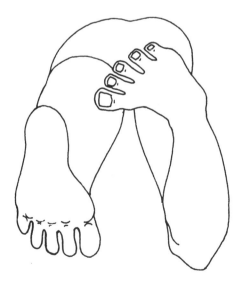

Fig 19   Flexible human feet can act as a propeller.

The Mechanics of Swimming

described in the previous paragraph, the difference in pressure was kept in one place, by standing still and sculling, and the pressure difference resulted in a vortex. Inspection of photographs and films taken underwater very often reveals swirls and rings, but because the hands and feet are moving all the time, a vortex will not appear.

Flexibility (Figs 20 & 21)

Flexible ankles and feet are valuable assets in swimming all strokes. When a person sits on the floor with the legs extended side by side, knees braced straight, it is possible to drop the feet until they are in line with legs. If the legs are moved apart and then rotated inwards, the feet will drop, until the toes touch the floor. This rotation of the legs is a counterpart of the arm rotation in sculling with the hands, to have the thumb up for the inward press and the little finger up for the outward press. It is to be seen in all strokes, including the breaststroke, where the very best swimmers end their leg kick with a foot swirl which brings the big toes together just as the thumbs are on top as the hands move in when sculling. Once again it seems to be a movement adopted by those with the necessary flexibility and the natural feel for the propulsion induced.

For those with less flexible ankles and feet, the legs have to be moved further apart to permit their inward rotation and, unhappily for some, lack of flexibility means that they cannot produce this desirable foot swirl with its change of pitch. They must rely on Newton's third law.

Summary

It must be repeated that lift, or thrust, deriving from Bernoulli principles will only happen when the hands or feet are moving at the speed appropriate for the individual. Swim-

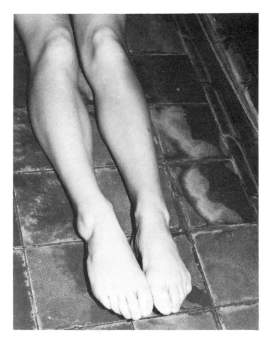

Fig 20   Plantar flexed feet with the legs held close together.

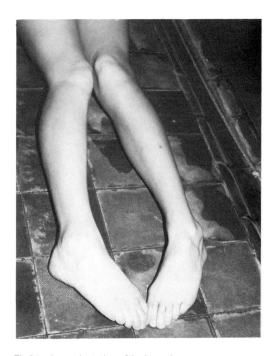

Fig 21   Inward rotation of the legs gives greater foot extension. In-toeing is seen in all excellent leg kicks.

mers will employ combinations of Newtonian mechanics and Bernoulli principles according to their physical build, strength, skill and natural feel for the water. It has been stated that all the young swimmers in one club who have been taught to scull properly, are able to create a vortex and as a consequence are swimming better because of this practice.

TEACHING SEQUENCES

The description of the four recognised strokes will follow the sequences used in teaching them. At one time breaststroke was always taught first, but today freestyle, or frontcrawl, is usually tackled first and as soon as the learner is moving, backcrawl is started. Full use is made of dog-paddle, sometimes called front paddle, and of back-paddle, or back sculling.

At this point usually breaststroke is introduced, swum on the front or the back, and the swimmer then develops rapidly on the stroke favoured most, but continues to develop the others. The method is well known and aptly named 'multi-stroke' and is far better than the rigid teaching of one stroke only. Eventually butterfly is taught, and for many years experienced teachers have waited until the frontcrawl is well mastered before introducing butterfly.

A new, younger generation of teachers has arrived which questions the established beliefs and who are introducing butterfly quite successfully after the initial frontcrawl–backcrawl sequence. It is claimed that the butterfly kick follows logically from the crawl kick, as does the overwater arm recovery. It is further claimed that the simultaneous movement of arms and of legs in butterfly transfers well to breaststroke, so that there is less difficulty with unequal or uneven limb movements.

Probably there is little difference between the two sequences, but they are worthy of more than a passing thought. In this work, the detailed description of the four strokes will be in the order frontcrawl, backcrawl, butterfly and finally breaststroke.

COMMON SWIMMING FACTORS *(Fig 22)*

The illustration shows the outline of a swimmer approaching head-on. The lower arms are in different positions to illustrate long lever and short lever action. Both arms are to be considered as being in the same plane as the shoulders.

The muscles from the chest wall and the back, which attach to the upper arm, work most effectively at the angle shown. In all the four recognised strokes, talented swimmers adopt positions showing that angle, regardless of body roll, body position on front or back, and the long or short lever position of the lower arm.

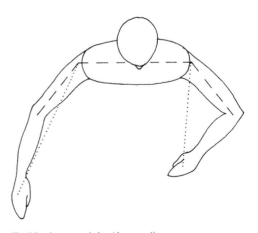

Fig 22   Long and short lever action.

2 Frontcrawl

INTRODUCTION

Freestyle is precisely what its name implies, namely a stroke that may be swum as the performer wishes, but it must be remembered that other countries have stricter interpretations than exist in Great Britain.

Frontcrawl is a more accurate name than freestyle for the stroke that is the fastest of all. Its characteristics are that the swimmer is on the front and rolling. The legs are under the water, kicking up and down alternately with the toes pointed, and the arms also work alternately under the water, but recover through the air. The swimmer's face is in the water, turning to the side for breathing, a movement neatly fitted into the action of the arms.

In describing a stroke in general terms, or for an individual performer, it is customary to follow a pattern:

1. Body position.
2. Leg action.
3. Arm action.
4. Breathing.
5. Timing.

Body position is placed first, because if the body is not in the most favourable swimming position for the individual, then it must be adjusted before all else.

Leg action is traditionally second, as it is a function of the leg kick to hold the body in a good swimming position, as well as to provide some propulsion.

Arm action is third, as the arms are the main source of propulsion, except in most cases of breaststroke swimming, but the arms cannot work properly until the body is maintained in a swimming position by an effective leg kick.

Breathing comes fourth, because distance swimming and speed swimming, apart from comfort, will not develop until an economical breathing technique, which does not interfere with the stroke, has been acquired.

Timing, sometimes referred to as 'co-ordination', is last because it is a description of the way in which the other four items are integrated into a complete stroke.

It should be observed that some experienced teachers and coaches prefer to have arm action second, because the arms are usually the main propulsive source, and to place the leg kick third. Whichever system is adopted, the process is called analysis and is a quick, convenient method of setting down a stroke.

Technique and Style

At this point, too, it should be made clear as to what is meant by *technique* and by *style*. Technique is the application of basic principles of swimming, which are universal, because all over the world people swim best with their bodies in a streamlined position and by pushing their hands towards their feet, for example. Style is an individual's personal interpretation of technique, so that two people could each have immaculate technique, with widely diverging styles. Good teachers and coaches have learned not to be rigid in their attitudes, but to allow individual differences to mature. It would be a poor teacher or coach who expected all the swimmers in his care to be identical in their performance.

ANALYSIS *(Figs 23 to 30)*

Body Position

'The frontcrawl swimmer's body position is flat and streamlined.' Such a statement is heard on the poolside and seen in sporting literature, but it is a half-truth. Viewed from the side, the body does remain straight and streamlined, as it does when seen from directly above. From a head-on viewing, however, it can be seen at once that there is considerable rolling, well controlled by skilled performers.

Breathing in frontcrawl involves turning the head to the side, so that streamlining is maintained as the breath is taken. Body roll aids the turning movement of the head. The arm action of the stroke is one with recovery over the water and rolling of the body lifts the recovering shoulder and arm, which eases the recovery movement, particularly for those people who are stiff in the shoulders. The degree of roll will therefore reflect the physical characteristics of an individual, for a muscular, short-necked, stiff shouldered person will roll up to 70 degrees or more in order to breath and to recover the arms comfortably and efficiently. Those people with poor floating ability and who are therefore low in the water, will also roll considerably, but those who float high and who have a flexible neck and shoulders, will not need to employ so much rolling.

Head Position

From the side, it can be seen that the majority of swimmers adjust the head position so that the water line is cut by the forehead, but it can be cut by the eyebrows, or by the crown of the head. Should a swimmer's hips be high enough to be above water level, or should the feet be lifting clear of the water and causing excessive splash, adjustment of the head position is a remedy, as it lowers the hips and the feet. The eyes look forward and downward, but for beginners it is better to suggest that the nose points forward and downward, because the nose is a fixed point, whereas young children might well move their eyes without adjusting the vital head position.

Shoulders

The shoulders will be as high as personal buoyancy allows, so that some will have a low position and others the advantage of a higher one. The shoulders should not be higher than the head, although learners are sometimes seen with their heads buried in the water and their shoulders humped, probably believing that they are achieving greater speed.

Hips

Stable hips is a phrase meaning that the hips remain high and in the same relative position, so that hip stability is a sign of sound swimming. The opposite is true as well, because when control of the hips is lost, they start to sink, which means that the swimming position is also lost and resistance increases rapidly. It takes only a moment to look at a very good exponent of frontcrawl to see the apparent 'dry triangle' formed by the shoulders as the base and the two longer sides running down to the point where the spine joins the pelvis. The hips also roll at the same time as the shoulders, though usually slightly less, due to the flexibility of the spine. Those swimmers who lack flexibility will obviously roll more.

Viewed from above, the body should remain in a straight line, but deviations occur when the head is moved too far to one side and when the arm action is too wide of the shoulders, or the pathways followed by the arms, their limb tracks, cross each other under the water. The hands push towards the feet, which in turn react towards the hands, while the hips react away. When poor limb tracks are used, the excessive reactions are easily seen at the feet and hips.

Leg Action

Many joints exist in the human body, the largest being the hip, which is consequently served by groups of very strong muscles – the prime or main movers of the legs. English language has the saying 'put your back into it' and in such a position, the legs are placed so that the powerful muscles grouped around the hip are used. For this reason, all the crawl type kicks begin at the hip; frontcrawl, back-crawl and butterfly. Once the large muscles of the hip have initiated the kicking action, the lighter but still strong muscles of the leg continue it, so that the slow movement commenced at the hip is translated into an accelerating whip of the foot.

Kicking Action

The kicking action is largely an up and down movement, up and down relative to the swimmer's own body, for it must be remembered that the body is rolling up to 70 degrees, at which angle a large part of the kick will be in a sideways direction.

Those people with loose ankles and soft feet have an advantage, and many of them quite naturally employ *in-toeing,* where the leg is rotated inwardly so that the big toe points inwards. This makes the foot a more efficient flipper.

During the continuous kicking action, the feet pass close together, and in-toeing often places one above the other. This is a movement natural to many swimmers, who can cover long distances at good pace using their legs only for propulsion. The primary aim of the strong leg action is not propulsion, but to hold the hips up, maintaining a desirable body position for successful swimming. Variations in the kinds of kick will be dealt with later, but weak leg kicks derive from infringements of basic requirements.

Checkpoints

1. The kick must come from the hip. Weak kicks often start at the knee, employing weak muscles and not involving the powerful hip muscles.
2. The kick must be continuous. Development of a sound, continuous leg action precedes many others. A learner will spend much time swimming legs only, with a float or kickboard supporting the body, until a continuous kick is established and can be maintained.
3. The kick must be effective. It will be effective when the hips are held in a high, stable position.

An observant teacher or coach will look tolerantly on a pupil who is having difficulty with learning the frontcrawl leg action. They should look specifically at ankle mobility and at the relative lengths of the upper and lower legs. If the upper leg is longer than the lower, then a long lever is moving a short lever, which is mechanically an advantage. However, if the upper leg is shorter than the lower, a short lever is moving a long lever, which is a disadvantage. It takes little imagination to picture the difficulties of a person with adverse upper to lower leg lengths and stiff ankles as well. Such a person will have to depend on arm action much more than most in order to swim frontcrawl, and will find leg kick exercises or drills exhausting and unprofitable.

Arm Action

Arm action is sub-divided into distinct parts, though it is performed as a continuous skilled movement.

Entry

Entry is the point where the hand is placed in the water, which is somewhere between the swimmer's centre line and the shoulder line. It should not be wide of the shoulder line, nor across the centre line. A moment's reflection on the streamlined position of a diver's arms will show that an entry position on, or close to, the centre line is desirable. A wide entry causes unwanted resistance.

Some swimmers employ a long entry, reaching well forward before sliding the hand in, while others use a short entry, sliding the hand into the water and then extending the arm to push the hand forward. Probably, the long or short entry is a natural choice reflecting the swimmer's individual buoyancy. A good floater has time to reach forward, but a less buoyant swimmer will get the arm back into the water to gain maximum flotation as early as possible.

During entry, the elbow is higher than the hand, some swimmers having the elbows peaked sharply and others having a gentle slope from elbow to fingertips. It is a very important part of technique to ensure that the slope exists and, as a generalisation, it can be said that the 'elbow high' entry leads to good arm action underwater. The hand slides into the water fingertips first and it usually is pitched, or angled, so that the little finger is higher than the thumb. Pitching the hand keeps the elbow high and gives minimum splash on entry.

Poor entries are made with a dropped elbow, meaning that the elbow is lower than the hand, which tends to slap the water, or

with a straight arm which smashes violently into the water. A dropped elbow puts the arm and shoulders in a position where the muscles around the shoulder joint work inefficiently. A smash entry drags large air bubbles into the water, and truly good swimming is made difficult if the water is alive with air, which reduces the grip normally attainable.

Catch (Fig 31)

Catch is the point at which the hand begins to exert pressure on the water and this should be as early as possible, usually about eight inches or twenty centimetres below the surface. A teacher or coach checking a pupil's progress will ensure that the elbow is still higher than the hand and that the hand is shaped to press on the water. The arm is extended, but not straight or stiff.

Pull

The pull phase of arm action develops from the catch point, as the hand accelerates due to the bending of the elbow and the arm pressing downwards, moved by the powerful muscles around the shoulder. It will be recalled that some people swim with long levers, or long arms, but that even so, there will be some elbow flexion. The very best frontcrawlers bend the elbow up to 90 degrees, but whatever degree of bending is utilised, it is at a maximum when the hand, elbow and shoulder are level. Should the elbow be leading at this point, then a weaker action is the result. The elbow should be high, and all through the pull phase, the hand is said to be catching the elbow.

Throughout this phase, good swimmers will have changed the pitch of their hands, as well as their acceleration, to attain thrust from Bernoulli principles. The hand passes underneath the face.

Fig 23 The left arm at entry, with its elbow
        higher than the hand. Note the degree
        of overlap between the arms, with the
        right arm just about half-way through
        its action.

Fig 25 A different angle, showing the left arm
        balanced by the upkick of the right leg.
        Note the in-toeing.

Fig 24 The left arm stretches to catch point,
        aided by body roll, which helps the
        right arm to lift clear of the water.

Fig 26 The hand presses back and down as
        the elbow flexes.

Fig 29   Acceleration is highest for the last
          movement, which presses the hand
          beyond the costume line.

Fig 27   From this angle, it is easier to see that
          the hand is pressing close to the
          centre line of the body. The right hand
          is just breaking the surface.

Fig 28   At this point the arm is straightening.
          Note where the eyes are looking and
          the nose is pointing.

Fig 30   Entry position with a long arm, little
          finger slicing in without a trail of air
          bubbles. The body is in the water, with
          only the crown of the head above the
          surface. Compare the general line of
          the body with that of a gymnast
          performing a handstand and with a
          diver in flight.

Frontcrawl

Fig 31   The swimmer stands at shoulder depth and imitates the teacher's demonstration of bent arm position at the end of the pull and start of the push, learning that the hand, elbow and shoulder are all level.

Push

The push phase is the final underwater movement, as the elbow is straightened powerfully and the angle of the wrist is continuously adjusted so that the palm of the hand faces backwards as much as possible. The acceleration of the hand takes it to its maximum underwater speed and its pitch is also altered. Much of the push phase is underneath the body, but finally the hand moves outwards in order to clear the hips. During the push phase, the arm is attaining a more streamlined position close to the body and as the very best frontcrawlers have the best push phases, unlike weak swimmers who fail to push right through, if they push at all, it is not difficult to conclude that this is the most important phase for speed.

Checkpoints

At this stage it is worth linking the three underwater sections of arm action, with a teaching or coaching instruction attached.

1. Catch point. Roll and press. Roll the body towards the working hand which presses firmly and strongly on the water.
2. Pull phase. Press and bend. Continue to press, but bend the arm, keeping the elbow high.
3. Push phase. Push right through. Continue to press, until you feel your thumb brush your

leg below the edge of your swim suit.

Some swimmers almost straighten their arms, but most, particularly sprint swimmers, do not fully extend them, keeping the elbow slightly flexed.

Recovery (Figs 32 & 33)

Recovery starts below the water directly propulsion ceases, and this part of the action is sometimes referred to as the *release,* or how the hand is taken out of the water. For most swimmers, it is a continuation of the elbow flexion at the end of the push phase. The body is then rolling towards the arm working underwater and away from the recovering arm, so

the elbow flexion and roll combine to lift the arm and shoulder clear of the water.

From the point of release of the hand from the water, two recovery actions can be initially considered. In one, the elbow is well peaked, bringing the relaxed recovering hand close alongside the body as it moves forward, with its fingertips just above the water surface. This is known as a high elbow recovery and should not be confused with the similar terminology used to describe the underwater high elbow action in the pull phase. The other recovery is with small elbow flexion and with an extended arm describing a large circle in a swinging movement, usually with the little finger uppermost so that the back of the hand faces forward. This is known as a ballistic recovery,

Fig 32 Ballistic arm recovery, but with the elbow higher than the hand, which has the little finger up. Note the angle of roll. This is late breathing with the arm well through recovery and the mouth still open to take the breath.

Fig 33 Straight arm recovery in frontcrawl,
with the hand higher than the elbow.

which is used by those with less flexible shoulders.

Between the high elbow and the ballistic recoveries there exist many variations and combinations. There are swimmers who employ what is known as a semi-ballistic recovery, a term implying a position half-way between the two. Some swimmers recover one arm with a high elbow and the other ballistically. Once again, the swimmer's choice reflects largely the individual's personal buoyancy and flexibility.

The ballistic recovery, with its high energy swinging action is the cause of reactions at the feet which will be dealt with under 'timing' later.

Whichever recovery is used, it ends as the fingertips slide smoothly into entry to start the whole process again. Recovery through the air meets less resistance than exists for the propulsive underwater phase and there is an amount of catch up, which is lost once the arm is in the water. Normally as one arm is at entry, the other is well through its propulsive phase, but some swimmers have what is called a 'catch-up' stroke, when both arms are in front of the body together. One arm rests in the catch position while the other goes through its propulsive phase, and then recovers to enter and to catch, when it in turn rests while its partner works. The amount of overlap varies, but swimmers who use this style have, in common, an outstandingly efficient leg kick.

Regardless of the efficiency of the leg kick, the main propulsion in frontcrawl derives from the alternating arm action.

Breathing *(Figs 34 to 37)*

For this work, breathing is defined as moving air out of and into the lungs. In swimming, it should interfere not at all or as little as possible with the stroke. Most physical exercise involves timing the breathing with the action and the heavier the strain, usually, the louder the grunts, as the breath is first held, then released under pressure from the build-up in the lungs and from the powerfully contracting muscles.

Frontcrawl employs the very mobile shoulder joint, with its powerful muscles situated on the chest and back. The face is in the water, for periods between breaths, which causes a pressure build-up in the lungs as carbon dioxide is returned from the working tissues. The muscles of the chest are working to move the arms, so the best time to breathe is when one arm is at entry, or catch, about to start its action and the other is recovering. This is the non-propulsive phase and is also the time of maximum acceleration when, in any stroke, it is the ideal moment to breathe.

One arm is forward, waiting to start its work, and the other is recovering. The swimmer relaxes the muscles restricting breathing, so that air leaks from the nose and mouth. Some teachers and coaches make too much of this, and if the stream of bubbles seen from a pin-hole puncture when an air-bed or an inner tube is placed in water is considered, then obviously the leakage is but a very small part of the total. The head is turned to the chosen side and the mouth opened wide, so that the air is expelled forcefully. If forceful breathing is performed on dry land, the contents of the abdomen can be felt pushing against the diaphragm, the main respiratory muscle. This breathing action is called 'explosive', an apt term to convey the speed with which up to five litres of air are driven out and then five litres more taken in.

Although the head is turned to the side at the time of expiration and inspiration, it is often below the general level of the water, because the speed of swimming generates a wave immediately in front of the swimmer's head with a trough behind it, conveniently placed for breathing. It is a skilled action and takes time to develop.

Once breathing is completed, the head is rotated so that the face is back in the water, and meanwhile the legs have continued kicking and the arms have moved on in their actions. Nothing stops, and the explosive breathing of a well-trained swimmer is measured in tenths of a second.

Some swimmers breathe naturally to their left and some to the right. They should learn both, and then a combination, called bilateral breathing, is available, when a breath is taken first to one side, then the breath is held and the next breath is taken on the opposite arm, thus reducing the total number of breaths taken in any given distance, and consequently the number of possible interruptions in the stroke cycle. It gives smoother performance, as the head is turned at every third stroke instead of every second.

The ideal time for breathing out and then immediately in, on the rebound as it were, is at the non-propulsive point of the stroke, when one arm is recovering. If this arm is seen to be well on its way forward when the mouth opens wide for maximum tidal airflow, then it is termed late breathing – late in the sense of the position of the recovering arm. It is like the hand of a clock. If the recovering hand, however, is still in its push phase, the swimmer is said to be breathing early. Late or early breathing may interfere with the stroke efficiency, but for some swimmers they are the natural consequence of a very effective leg kick, or a very powerful arm action.

In the pages on mechanics, attention was drawn to the buoyancy given by the air in the lungs, which is another reason for fast, explosive breathing. Slow breathing will interfere with the stroke cycle and reduce flotation. Breath holding, at certain stages in a race, such as the finish, is widely used, as it is in learning stroke timing.

Timing

Timing, often called co-ordination, describes how the arm and leg actions are related to each other and to the breathing action used. The usual co-ordination in a stroke cycle is six leg kicks to one arm cycle, aptly described as 'the classic six beat style'. One arm cycle is a complete action for each of the two arms, and six divided by two equals three, so that the working arm is balanced by the opposite leg, just as in walking or running. The six beat is seen usually with an efficient leg kick and with a high elbow recovery.

Another common co-ordination is the two beat, where there are two leg kicks to the arm cycle. It is associated with longer distances, so that one swimmer might well use six beat for sprinting, say over 50 metres, and two beat for a long swim, 400 metres for example, but in the finish of the longer race, could return to six beat. It is to be seen that some swimmers will use a six beat kick coming out of their turns and switch naturally to two beat timing as their arms start their movement. The two beat kick is associated with stiff ankles, when a minimum but balancing action is required, and with the ballistic recovery action mentioned earlier.

Close observation of the two beat reveals that the kick is wider apart than the six beat, usually about hip width, with distinct down kicks and then sometimes what is termed an up-float, as the leg slowly recovers before its next kick. If it is combined with the ballistic recovery, frequently the legs cross at the ankles between each kick. This is called a cross-over kick and if it happens on both legs, it is a double cross-over.

A rare form of timing is the four beat kick, and there are some swimmers who make so little use of their legs that they are said to swim with a trailing leg action, usually shortened to a trail. Another rare co-ordination involves the self-descriptive scissor kick, when the swimmer has rolled well to one side and the legs are opened in a large scissor movement, which is characteristic of slow breathing, when the movement of arms and legs is slowed or exaggerated by a long, slow out and in of breath.

A useful tip is to have swimmers with difficult and unusual actions to swim short distances without breathing. If the action in question disappears, it is a result of breathing. Should the unwanted action persist, the teacher or coach will know to look elsewhere.

This section on timing is best finished by observing that the three men who were first in the world to swim faster than 50 seconds for a 100 metres Freestyle used widely varying styles, their personal interpretations of basic mechanics. One used the classic six beat, one used a two beat, and the other used a catch-up.

Frontcrawl Pre-requisites
(Fig 38)

1. The ability to open the eyes under water.
2. The ability of aquatic breathing, which is to place the head in the water, then turn or lift it to breathe and, without pause, replace it in the water.
3. The ability to regain the feet from the horizontal prone position. Important for small children whose chins just clear the water.
4. The possession of watermanship, which is the ability of the swimmer to be aware of his position in the water, even with his face in the water, when the eyes and ears are shut off,

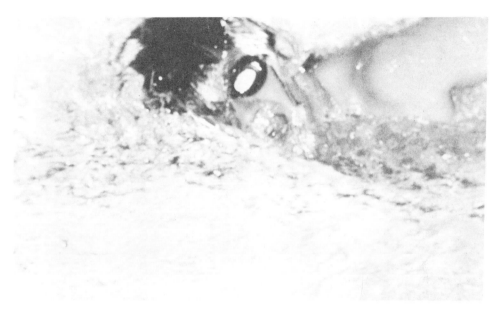

Fig 34   Lightning quick breathing.

Fig 35   This learner is practising turning the head, using a float for added buoyancy.

Frontcrawl

Fig 36 The head is turned so that the mouth
opens in a trough behind the bow
wave pushed up by the head.

Fig 37 A supporting arm is correctly placed
on the float as the swimmer performs
one-arm frontcrawl with the breathing
well timed.

and to retain this ability even when some fatigue sets in, or when water unexpectedly washes over the head. Good teachers will play lots of games to ensure watermanship.
5. The ability to swim dog-paddle, preferably extended dog-paddle, with its pull-push action.
6. The ability to kick efficiently using a float, with the head up or with the face in the water.

Teaching Frontcrawl

As in nearly all swimming, begin at the rail and transfer the exercise to the float as soon as possible to give the feeling of movement. Work through dog-paddle and stick to it until the learner has the pre-requisites listed earlier.

Exercises (Fig 39)

1. At the rail: kicking, face down. Lift one arm, whichever is favourite, and turn the head to that side to breath. If this is too difficult, perform the action standing in water, knees bent to have shoulders under water. Establish the natural breathing side by trial. Transfer this to the float.
2. At the rail: kicking face down; lift one hand off the rail and perform one complete arm action while breathing to that side. The hand must be placed back on the rail after breathing is over. Transfer this to the float. Stress that the hand on the breathing side must be replaced on the float after the breath has been taken.
3. On the float. Practise breathing to the favoured side until widths are achieved with

Fig 38   Confident breathing has the lips lifted no higher than necessary.

easy, continuous arm action.

4. Full stroke:

   (a) Swim widths without breathing.
   (b) Swim widths with one breath, taken half-way across.
   (c) Swim widths with two breaths, then three.
   (d) Build a continuous swim across the width with breaths taken every stroke to the natural side.

Coaching Frontcrawl

Frontcrawl is the workhorse of training, because it gives the greatest distance for the time involved. However, as with many human activities, over-use can be destructive. Over-familiarity leads to loss of learning. Excessive frontcrawl can harm it, ruining its feel of rhythm and power.

Break up the frontcrawl work. Use a wide range of distances, and of speeds. Use flippers and paddles, either singly or in combination. Use kickboards and pull-buoys to ease the demand. With older and more skilled swimmers, give them a choice of activity. With your stroke drills and skills, reinforce the basic analysis, but with allowance for individual differences.

1. Body position. Always state whether a drill is with head up or with head down. It has a different effect on the swimming position and on the heart rate.

2. Leg kick. Use deep kicking, as well as normal kicking. State whether the drill is to be swum head up or face down.

3. Arm action. Selected arm drills should

Fig 39 Frontcrawl leg action by a learner using two floats for a safe, stable position.

stress the various phases of action, depending on where the arm starts. If it is at the catch, then the roll and press into pull and push will be emphasised. If it starts at the side, the recovery, with high elbow will be stressed.

4. Breathing.

(a) Breathe to the right on one length, to the left on the next and so on.

(b) Breathe three to the right, then three to the left, or vary the number.

(c) Bilateral breathing for distance swims.

(d) Breath holding should be used with caution, particularly with younger swimmers. Underwater training exercises need the same caution.

Many years of patience are required to produce a mature frontcrawl swimmer.

3 Backcrawl

INTRODUCTION

Any stroke swum on the back is a form of backstroke, of which backcrawl is one. Old English backstroke uses a breaststroke type leg kick, with a double arm action involving an overwater recovery, though it can also be swum with the arms recovering at the side of the body and in the water, for part of their return. Life-saving leg kick uses a breaststroke type leg action as well, and the hands may scull at the sides of the body, aiding propulsion, or are free for any life-saving skills. Back-paddle, or back sculling, the counterpart of front or dog-paddle, is a swimming skill in its own right, as well as an essential progression towards backcrawl. It is economical in its energy demands, once learned, and uses an alternating crawl kick, while the hands scull at the side of the hips.

Backstrokes are to be considered as resting strokes, because the majority of swimmers, even powerful ones, will turn on to the back for a respite at demanding times, to have the face clear of the water. The main disadvantage of backstroke is that the swimmer is unable to see the way ahead, unless the head is turned at an awkward and uncomfortable angle. Generally, all swimming is remarkably free of accidents, but it is the backstroke swimmers who tend to collect the most bumps, on the head or hand. During the teaching stages, teachers should take great care to ensure that learners look to see that the way is clear before swimming, and that the class or group is organised in such a way that collisions are avoided. At coaching level, one of the most painful knocks occurs when a

backcrawler pushes off hard, in a racing start or turn, as another swimmer approaches the end of the pool. Older swimmers involved in this level of training learn to take care, but one of the tasks always with the coach is safe lane organisation for backcrawl training.

This section will deal with backcrawl, which is characterised by the alternating leg kick and the alternating arm action with overwater recovery, while the swimmer is face upwards. Close study of films, or of actual swimmers, shows that good backcrawl is never swum flat on the back, because the body obviously rolls. Swimming law allows the swimmer to roll up to 90 degrees each way. In other words, if the body is not on its front, then it must be on its back.

ANALYSIS *(Figs 41 to 50)*

Body Position *(Fig 51)*

When viewed from the side, the body assumes a shallow dish shape, which is similar to that used by good gymnasts in handstands. It is a strong position. The head is held slightly up, as though resting on a cushion, and the phrase 'head pillowed on the water' is accurate and descriptive. The actual head angle adopted by a person will depend on individual physical characteristics, as raising the head higher will cause the feet to drop, while pushing it back raises them. If the head is held out of the water, as learners are apt to do, it causes the hips to drop and an unacceptable swimming position is the result. During backcrawl swimming, the head remains very steady, and it is this appearance which leads unquestioning observers to assume that the body has the same steadiness, when in reality good technique requires body roll.

Normal limits of head position will have the nose pointing somewhere between straight up, and to an angle of approximately 45 degrees away from the vertical towards the feet.

The shoulders are high and the hips are also well up to the surface, but not as high as in frontcrawl. Leg action has alternating flexion and extension of the knee, but the knee should not break the surface. Flexion is greater than in frontcrawl, because the foot is dropping downwards. (Should the same degree of flexion be employed in frontcrawl then the feet would lift clear of the water.) The feet kick up to the surface, but too much splash is indicative of poor swimming and the toes should just lift to, but not break, the surface.

When viewed from head-on, it is apparent that there are two extreme styles, one using a position with the line of the shoulders remaining parallel to the surface of the water, and the other with the shoulders rolling so that the shoulder line assumes an angle of up to 70 degrees to the left and to the right. Between these two extremes, every possible variation can be found.

The hips and feet roll with the body, so that a large component of the kick is sideways at certain moments, and not simply up and down in a vertical plane. It is to be observed that some swimmers roll the shoulders more than the hips, while others roll the body as one unit.

Fig 40   Learners using backcrawl sculling
         have their hips low, but the leg kick is
         coming nicely. Photographs of the
         best swimmers show that most of the
         body is underwater.

Backcrawl

Fig 41 The entry with little finger down and no air bubbles trailing, which is highly desirable.

Fig 44 The hand starts to rise due to the elbow flexion. The fingers are pointing sideways.

Fig 42 The elbow has started to bend.

Fig 43 The elbow flexion increases. The fingers are pointing down.

Fig 45 The elbow has its greatest angle of bend.

Fig 46   Half-way through the arm action, with
         hand, elbow and shoulder all level.
         The hand has caught up with the
         elbow at the end of the pull.

Fig 47   The hand has led the elbow into the
         push phase. The depth of the
         shoulder reveals the degree of roll.

Fig 48   The hand faces backwards, fingers
         pointing up. At this point the hand is
         accelerating to its highest speed.

Fig 49   The hand flips down as the opposite
         hand enters. Note the position of the
         right foot balancing the left arm.

Fig 50   A final push down, well below the
         body, which keeps the hips up and
         aids the roll to the other side for the
         arm about to work there.

Backcrawl

Fig 51   A gymnast shows a strong straight position. This can be seen in diving, frontcrawl and backcrawl, with slight changes in the head position.

Leg Action

As in all crawl type kicks, with pointed toes, the kick originates at the hip, utilising the powerful muscles grouped there. Once the inertia of the limb is overcome by these muscles, the action passes to the leg muscles, which straighten the knee and produce the accelerating movement which ends in the whip-like movement of the foot. In-toeing is beneficial and, though the feet pass side by side, the in-toeing achieved by inward rotation of the leg will for many swimmers place one foot directly above the other. The action is continuous and provides excellent propulsion, but its main consequence is to hold the hips in a steady position, maintaining an acceptable swimming shape.

Some difficulties are commonly met, deriving from individual physical attributes, such as leg length and ankle stiffness, already dealt with in the pages on frontcrawl. For such people, backcrawl may be even more difficult, because all backcrawl swimmers need a fine leg kick. The weaker, or less skilled the kick, the harder it is to retain a swimming position and the stroke becomes very difficult.

For beginners, fear may be an element in their approach, because it is not possible to see the way ahead, and if the head sinks, water rushes into the eyes and nose and perhaps the mouth. Timid approaches to backcrawl are signalled by the learner keeping one leg much lower than the other, ready to put it on the bottom if needed, so that only one leg is used for propulsion. If the head is held high, the hips drop, placing the body in a poor swimming position by forcing the legs low in the water.

Another common difficulty is kicking from the knees, or using a bicycle riding action, instead of kicking from the hips. This can be identified easily, as the knees break the surface, and may be put right in several ways. A

From head-on, it can be seen that the feet react towards the working arm and the hips away from it, so that as the right arm acts, the feet move to the right and the hips to the left. Because the arm action is of necessity further from the centre line of the body than it is in frontcrawl, the reactions are more marked. It is called *lateral deviation.*

This deviation is most easily seen from directly above. Good technique minimises it, but beginners may have a snaking action, sometimes made worse by moving the head from side to side. It is good teaching to tell beginners to imagine that there is a glass of milk balanced on the forehead and to try to swim without spilling it.

float, or kickboard, can be held at such a length that it covers the knees, keeping them down, while the teacher emphasises 'long legs', 'kick your socks off', and older beginners can be told that it is the feet which push you along, not the knees.

It cannot be over-emphasised that a sound, well-established leg kick is essential for backcrawl swimming and that no attempt should be made to proceed to the arm action until the learner has achieved the required level of competence.

Arm Action *(Figs 52 & 53)*

There are two extremes of body position, when the view is from head-on. One has the shoulder line staying generally parallel with the surface of the water, and the other with the shoulder line rolling up to 70 degrees.

Mechanically, all human movement re-quires the use of short levers (flexion) and long levers (extension) alternately. In swimming, the great range of movement available at the shoulder, coupled with elbow flexion, makes the arms powerful, more so in frontcrawl than in backcrawl, where the latter imposes restrictions on the range of mobility.

When these two facts are linked, it can be understood that keeping the shoulders relatively flat means that a long arm must be used, or the hand would protrude from the water as the elbow bends. With shoulder roll, the arm deep in the water can bend up to 90 degrees safely, ensuring a powerful flexion and extension at the elbow. The speed of such a movement, joined with pitching of the hand, also ensures use of Bernoulli principles. It is of interest to note the range of shoulder positions adopted by swimmers. The small shoulder roll with a long arm may be likened to the

Fig 52   Bent arm action, showing body roll and an interesting use of inner range arm flexion.

Fig 53   Straight arm action revealing little body roll. The fingers are spread wide, which does not reduce the area. It happens as a natural reaction when stiffening of the wrist is needed.

Backcrawl

pace and action of an afternoon stroll, and the large shoulder roll with a well-flexed elbow to the pace and action of a track sprinter.

These two extremes are referred to as *long arm backcrawl* and *bent arm backcrawl*, which is rather misleading because the same distinctions are observable in all swimming. The more leisured long arm action tends to be adopted by those who have no need of hurry, while the more productive bent arm action is used by those in search of speed. It must be remembered that the power used to produce speed is also useful in giving economy of effort so that mechanically sound techniques for all strokes should be attempted by all learners.

Entry

The point at which the hand enters the water will depend on personal characteristics and on the technique used. Entries between the swimmer's own centre line and shoulder line are acceptable, preferably closer to the centre line, which should not be crossed. Knowledgeable teachers and coaches make allowance for any lateral deviation before pronouncing exactly where one particular swimmer enters his hand, and they also know that one swimmer may have different entry points for each hand. Absolute symmetry is rare in all strokes.

At entry, the arm is stretched but not stiff, and the shoulder is elevated as when reaching up to a shelf, but over-extension of any joint places it in a weak mechanical position and needs to be watched in advanced teaching and coaching. The hand is turned palm outwards so that the little finger enters first, with minimum splash, as the arm brushes the ear on that side of the head. (The body is rolling to the same side.) Some people who are stiff in the shoulders find it difficult to achieve this, and enter the hand either pitched to a greater or lesser angle, and some enter the hand palm

upwards, the backcrawl equivalent of the frontcrawl 'smash' entry.

Rolling of the body facilitates an entry closer to the centre line and also enables the swimmer to turn the hand palm downwards, or at least part downwards and sideways, as the arm and hand sink to the catch position.

Catch Position

Long arm action, with little body roll, has a catch position some 6 to 8 inches (15–20 cm) below the surface with the palm facing outwards. The total movement of the arm will be a long semi-circular one, but initially it is with the palm facing outwards. For every action there is an equal opposite reaction, so lateral deviation will be marked.

Bent arm action, with large body roll, has the hand facing largely downwards towards the bottom of the pool, so that skilled backcrawl swimmers exert a downward press on the water very early in the arm action, as in all strokes. It is more likely to be omitted from backcrawl than all other strokes, and teachers and coaches are heard giving the instruction to 'roll and press' in endeavours to include an early pressure in their swimmers' repertoires of skills.

Pull Phase

Those using the long arm action will have a little elbow flexion which happens in the pull phase, but generally by the time the arm is level with and at right angles to the shoulder, the arm remains long but lacks adequate acceleration. A long lever moves more slowly than a short lever. The palm is facing directly backwards, but is not moving at the pace and angle to use Bernoulli principles. Competitive swimmers using this action have achieved speeds which many weaker swimmers might envy, but they are fated to have limited speed unless their technique is changed.

Worst of the long arm actions is that where the swimmer lets the arm circle downwards as well as outwards in a deep pull, deeper than the hips, in contrast to the shallow semi-circular action described in the previous paragraph. This deep, scooping action places the shoulder in a very poor mechanical position, with little or no use of some of the powerful muscles available. When the hand is opposite the shoulder, it is at its deepest.

Bent arm action involves a technique common to all skilled swimming. From catch point, the hand presses downwards, as already described, before the elbow bends, pulling the hand closer to the centre line and with the hand turning to have the palm facing backwards. Due to the rolling of the body, at the end of the pull phase the elbow is at maximum flexion of up to 90 degrees, and the hand and elbow are both level with each other and with the shoulder. The hand has been accelerating since its entry and is at its highest point, with fingertips a few inches below the surface.

Push Phase

Use of the long arm action produces little push as there is little flexion of the elbow. (The powerful, accelerating push only occurs if there is sufficient flexion.) In this action, the arm and hand continue in a large semi-circle, with the palm facing more and more towards the swimmer's thigh, where the movement ends, having achieved insufficient acceleration and a reaction to one side.

Where the deep, scooping action below the body is used, from its position at the end of the first half of the underwater movement, the hand continues in a long, slow arc to bring it alongside the thigh, sometimes with the palm up. The law of action and reaction will cause the hips to move down.

Employment of bent arm action places the arm and hand in an ideal position at the end of the pull phase, with the elbow well flexed and the palm facing backwards. A powerful accelerating push occurs as the elbow is straightened and the arm extends close down the side of the body, where it also gives far less resistance. The final movement, as the hand changes its pitch, is a strong push towards the bottom of the pool, which aids propulsion and the rolling of the body towards the other arm. The speed and pitch of the hand allow application of Bernoulli principles, which combine with the low resistance position of the arm to give speed and economy of effort.

Recovery

The long arm action, in a shallow semi-circle, ends with the palm of the hand alongside the thigh, thumb uppermost. A similar position may occur at completion of the least desirable long arm action, in a deep semi-circle, but this kind of arm action may end with the palm up, in which case rotation of the arm will bring the thumb uppermost.

The bent arm action leaves the hand well below the surface, palm down, so recovery begins from this situation. Some swimmers simply lift the arm straight up and the hand emerges with its back uppermost. Others rotate the arm outwards and lift simultaneously to bring the hand out with its thumb uppermost and palm facing inwards. A third option is to rotate the arm inwards, so the hand breaks surface with the little finger on top and the palm facing outwards.

After breaking the surface, the recovery movements of the different underwater actions are similar. The arm is lifted straight up without crossing the swimmer's body or moving to one side. Crossing the body may cascade water onto a learner's face and cause discomfort. Moving the arm away to one side leads to an entry wide of the shoulder, which is also undesirable. At some time in this movement, the arm must be rotated so that the little finger leads backwards and the palm is facing outwards. This rotation unlocks the shoulder joint and permits a full movement which would not be possible with the thumb leading and the palm facing inward.

Hence, there are a number of reasons for recovering the arm with the palm facing outwards and the little finger leading:

1. The hand breaks the surface cleanly on release.
2. The shoulder joint is unlocked.
3. The shoulder of the recovering arm is lifted clear of the water, thus reducing resistance.
4. The hand is shaped ready for entry.

From the highest position above the shoulder, the hand accelerates to entry and to repeat its underwater propulsive action.

Breathing

It is said that breathing in backcrawl is no problem because the face is clear of the water. This takes no account of the fact that some of the muscles around the chest, front and back, also steady the shoulder joint, or are very active in the powerful, fast arm action required. If breathing takes place at the wrong time, it may well interfere with the stroke. A number of mechanically poor movements derive from a relaxation of the chest wall when it needs to be firm. Most obvious of these is the bent arm which is seen in recovery.

Most backcrawl swimmers breathe out as one arm finishes its underwater effort, and in as the other finishes. A few breathe out and immediately in again as the favoured arm ends its propulsion. Because the face is clear of the water, backcrawl breathing is frequently semi-explosive.

With beginners, in the earliest stages of swimming on the back, it is worth watching their breathing closely. If the mouth is closed, or nearly so, look at their nostrils, which may be seen closing and opening a small amount. Nose breathing is insufficient to move the quantities of air required, and all beginners on all strokes should be encouraged to open the mouth wide and force the air out and in strongly. Remember that breathing out must come before breathing in, and that back-stroke swimmers may not be able to see where they are going, but they are able to see you and to receive a mimed instruction.

Timing

Earlier it was emphasised that all back-crawlers must have an efficient leg kick. Those unable to develop such a kick turn to other strokes, so timing in backcrawl is usually very simple. There is one complete arm cycle to six leg kicks and, as in frontcrawl, two arm actions divided into six leg kicks gives three, which means that a leg is always balancing the opposite arm, as in walking. A four beat kick is found, but it is rare, with its slow, deep leg movement.

Should you wish to check your own or another swimmer's timing, consider either hand as it enters the water, when it should be balanced by the opposite leg with the toes just popping up.

Backcrawl Pre-requisites

1. The ability to regain the feet from a supine position.
2. The ability to accept water splashed on the face, as against being able to place the head in the water. (Teachers will be sympathetically aware of the small number of beginners who choose to swim on the back in order to avoid placing the face in the water.)
3. The ability to swim back-paddle.

4. The ability to be able to turn from the back onto the front and continue swimming.

Teaching Backcrawl *(Fig 54)*

Non-swimmers are able to feel what it is like to be on the back by holding on to the rail, or to the trough, raising their legs and body so that a semi-supine position is reached, and then pulling themselves along head first and having the sensation of the water flowing over the skin.

It is difficult and uncomfortable to learn backcrawl at the rail or trough. Progression is made from dog-paddle to back-paddle, using buoyancy aids to hold the body safely on the back while the leg kick is attempted. To this, sculling with one or both hands can be added and, as confidence and skill increase, the

buoyancy aid removed, until a true back-paddle results.

The arm action can be taught with the learner walking backwards and keeping the shoulders level with the water, before it is developed with one or both arms working, from the back-paddle. A useful method is to have the learner swim vigorously on back-paddle, sculling hard, and upon a signal or word from the teacher, to attempt the full arm action for a short distance. One-arm exercises, combined with use of a buoyancy aid, are most useful, as the learner can give full attention to the technique wanted.

Once the natural rhythm and technique are established, the distance swum is gradually increased, when backcrawl, because of its less demanding breathing technique, can be used to build up basic fitness for the other

Fig 54   A beginner using two floats to give
buoyancy in a wide stable position.
The mouth is closed, the hips are low
and a cycling action is bringing one
knee out of the water.

strokes.

Remember to encourage swimmers to 'roll and press'. Every teacher will have to face the choice of teaching long arm or bent arm action. For adult learners there is nothing wrong with long arm action in recreational swimming. Slow swimming involves low resistance.

Coaching Backcrawl

Backcrawl swimmers should have the competition turn flags available regularly for practice of accurate turning.

When the workhorse, frontcrawl, looks as if it is being flogged, backcrawl is an available substitute and many coaches, in a long, hard set of frontcrawl swims, will include a few backcrawl swims to break the tedium. Back-crawl should not be treated as a soft alternative, though. Over distance, backcrawl is harmless and much early fitness can be built with backcrawl, before turning to frontcrawl.

A common coaching error is to accept what swimmers do, instead of insisting positively on the way in which strokes and drills are performed. Show the swimmers exactly what is required of them in each drill, and see that it is obtained.

Backcrawl is a good choice for warm-up, particularly with younger swimmers who are still learning to spread their effort through a long training session. A swim-down on back-crawl at the conclusion of a demanding session is physiologically and psychologically sound practice.

4 Butterfly

INTRODUCTION

Butterfly is a powerful and handsome stroke when swum by a well-prepared swimmer, but many swimmers, teachers and coaches are shy of it because it appears to be demanding, both of the swimmer and of the instructor. There is little need for lack of confidence in coping with butterfly, as the new generations of swimmers and poolside helpers have grown up with it. Perhaps there is more need for caution from those who expect too much in performance from learners and those who treat the exertions of the stroke as a punishment.

In 1952, butterfly became the fourth recognised stroke, and now ranks second in speed behind the frontcrawl and before the backcrawl. Breaststroke butterfly combined a breaststroke leg kick with a double crawl arm action, and the legs and arms worked alternately, sometimes with a slight glide. It is not seen in competition at higher levels, though it remains a useful progression to dolphin butterfly for natural breaststroke swimmers and is a fun swim for short distances.

Since 1952 the dolphin butterfly has developed to its present level of performance for both women and men. It is governed by swimming laws which require the performer to:

1. Swim on the front with shoulders square.
2. Swim on the front with the shoulders horizontal.
3. Kick the legs simultaneously in a vertical plane.
4. Recover the arms simultaneously and symmetrically over the water.

5. Use the arms simultaneously and symmetrically under the water.

ANALYSIS *(Figs 55 to 62)*

Attention is drawn to the mechanics of flotation, where it has been stated that raising the arms above the water will cause the swimmer to sink, unless the swimmer opposes the down thrust with vigorous leg action. Raising the head and the shoulders also increases down thrust, which must be opposed. In swimming butterfly, there is a moment when the head and shoulders are raised to permit breathing, and the arms are recovered overwater, which forces the body down.

Once the mechanics of flotation are applied to butterfly, the characteristics of the stroke follow logically. Laws require the swimmer to remain on the front and, at some point, the breath must be taken, which raises the head and shoulders and lowers the legs. Laws require the arms to recover over the water and the down thrust needs a very powerful kick to counter it. The motion of the body, rising to permit a breath to be taken and then falling, derives from alternate downward and upward forces.

Stroke mechanics based on Newton's third law, state that every action produces an equal and opposite reaction and the hands, in pushing towards the feet to produce forward motion, also cause a reaction at the feet, which move towards the hands, and at the hips, which move away, reinforcing the rise and fall described in the previous paragraph, with the elegant undulation of well-swum

Butterfly

butterfly. In the early history of the stroke, this undulation was often exaggerated through misunderstanding of its mechanics, and learners today may well repeat that earlier error.

Body Position

From a side view, the undulation is seen to be controlled by skilled swimmers. Certainly the body rises and falls in a movement which is often greater on the breathing stroke, but the centres of gravity and buoyancy are given minimum displacement. It may be likened to a well-sprung car moving over a very bumpy road.

The head, on the non-breathing stroke, is held centrally with the face in the water and the water-level cutting the crown, very similar to its frontcrawl position, but often deeper. It is a useful teaching or coaching point to remind swimmers to look forward and downward, which positions the head correctly. Because the head is somewhat lower while the breath is held, the shoulders are that much relatively higher than in frontcrawl and, because the stroke is swum on the breast, without body roll, a slightly humpbacked position may be seen at certain points in the stroke cycle.

As already described, the hips rise, until the seat is close to the surface. Those who over-stress the movement may have the seat clearly out of the water. At the lowest point, the hips will sink to just beyond the body's own depth. Hip flexibility is needed and 'disco dancing' while standing in shoulder depth water is an interesting introduction to butterfly for those without natural feel for the undulation required.

Flexion of the knees is up to 90 degrees, the greatest angle of the crawl type leg actions and with this degree of bend, parts of the feet may break the surface.

During the breathing stroke, the head and shoulders rise until the chin is pushed forward by extending the neck. ('Push the chin forward' is another widely used teaching and coaching point.) The hips will sink lower and in this position, though the same degree of knee bend is made, the feet may not break the surface. Much depends upon personal physical factors, such as buoyancy and flexibility. In order to limit the undulations, the stroke is usually swum with alternating breathing and non-breathing strokes, called two-stroke breathing. The observant teacher or coach will note the differences in body position for an individual swimmer during the breathing cycle, as against the non-breathing cycle.

Undulation is unavoidable due to the mechanics already explained and if it could be 'averaged', it would be seen that the swimmer is endeavouring to hold as horizontal a position as possible.

Leg Action

In all strokes it is difficult to isolate one section, and this is particularly true of butterfly, where the body, legs, arms and breathing are closely integrated in their movements.

Swimming laws require the legs to kick up and down side by side, which they do in compensation for the upper body and arm movements. The double leg kick is initiated by the very powerful hip muscles, so that the tops of the feet and the legs press on the water partly downward and partly backwards. The backward component gives a forward reaction for propulsion, but the downward component lifts the upper body which is sinking due to arm recovery, with or without the head movement for breathing.

From their deepest point, the feet move up as the knees are bent and the hips sink. There is discussion as to whether this upward movement of the sole of the foot gives propulsion, in the butterfly or the frontcrawl and, similarly, in the downward movement in backcrawl. Should there be propulsion, it would be a small fraction of the reaction produced by the powerful hip and knee extension. Many skilled swimmers finish the down kick with inward rotation of the legs, producing the desirable in-toeing position.

Checkpoints

The leg action must be:

1. From the hip.
2. Continuous.
3. Simultaneous.
4. Effective.

If the hips lose stability, allowing the body position to deteriorate, then the kick is ineffective.

Arm Action

Entry

A diver holds the arms in a streamlined position to minimise resistance, and similarly a swimmer in frontcrawl and backcrawl, may enter one hand at the most advantageous point, the centre line. Some exceptionally flexible butterfly swimmers of high buoyancy and power are able to enter the hands close to the centre line, but usually the entry will be on the shoulder line, or inside it. An entry outside the shoulder line gives poor streamlining and is to be avoided.

The hands usually have a long entry, as the arms are long, but not rigid. Some swimmers have a short underwater extension of the hands and arms as seen in frontcrawl. Normally, the hands are entered pitched, with the thumbs down and the palms facing part downward and part outward. Shoulder flexibility will be an important factor in deciding the entry position, but whichever entry point is selected, the elbow must be higher than the hand.

Catch

Catch point, as in all skilled swimming, should be early. Less buoyant butterfly swimmers have a larger downward component to raise the upper body, but the hands also press out and back, with the elbow high. Beginners and tiring learners drop the elbow, so it will lead into a weak arm action.

Pull Phase

The hands press out, but are still moving backwards and downwards in a movement sometimes inaptly described as a double frontcrawl arm action, because it resembles more a breaststroke arm pull, when viewed from ahead, or from the side. During the accelerating movement, the hands change pitch so that at the completion of the pull phase, the palms are facing back and the hands, elbows and shoulders are all in line, an excellent position for a powerful push. Some swimmers will have their hands wider of the elbows than others, which reflects personal physical build.

Push Phase

There is no pause, but the hands push backwards and also move closer together, under the body, in an accelerating movement accompanied by a change of pitch in the hands. The distance between the hands as they push back is again a reflection of the performer's physical build, and it may be close enough for the thumbs nearly to touch, or almost the width of the body apart. The push must, however, be under the body and it continues to accelerate.

When the arms are nearly straight, with the

Butterfly

Fig 55 Entry position, showing the hands in line with the shoulders, thumbs down and elbows high. The head looks forward and down, and the legs are making the first balancing kick.

Fig 57 At this position the hands have almost caught the elbows. Note the pitch of the hands.

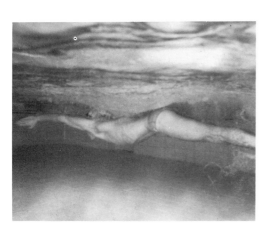

Fig 56 The arms pull outwards and backwards, with the elbow higher than the hands. The hips are lifted by the strong kick.

Fig 58 The hands move together, while still pressing back. Flexion at the knees prepares for the second kick.

Fig 59 The hands are close together, palms facing, in a powerful swirl.

Fig 61 At the end of the push phase, the hands, palms upward, are ready for the release. The balancing second kick is 'kicking the hands out'.

Fig 60 The push phase, with palms facing backwards and accelerating to maximum speed on the breathing stroke.

Fig 62 The hips sink due to arm recovery through the air and the head is returned to the water before the hand entry. The legs flex into recovery before 'kicking the hands in' and the hips up.

hands angled to face backwards, they swing out to clear the hips in preparation for release and recovery, after reaching maximum speed.

Pull-push Phases Combined

The limb tracks followed by the hands will be determined by their width apart at entry, the distance between them at the end of the pull phase, how close they are during their push phase and the width of the hips. Some swimmers have a pattern resembling a keyhole. Others have patterns variously described as an hour-glass or a wasp-waist, but the common factor is the one that produces movement, namely flexion, which is the pull phase, and extension, which is the push phase. The degree of flexion is a resultant of personal physique, strength and fitness.

The worst pull-push phase usually begins with an entry markedly wide of the shoulder line and the pull is made with a leading elbow; from here, there is little or no push. There are also swimmers who have a reasonable pull phase but who follow it with a push phase which is incomplete. It is an important point that will be taken up when discussing timing. A very wide entry, after which the hands pull in a straight line to their respective shoulders, is called a vee-pull.

Recovery (Figs 63 & 64)

Following the final acceleration in the push, the elbows flex to lift part of the arm clear of the water, as the arm rotates so that the hand

Fig 63 Butterfly arm recovery with the palms down. The palms should now be facing backwards with the little finger up. The head is late being returned to the water.

slices out of the water, little finger up, although some swimmers hold the hands palm up in a continuation of the push, and some have the thumb a little higher.

From here the arms swing in a fast, relaxed, circular movement, clearing the water. Swimmers fortunate in their buoyancy and flexibility, may keep the hands palm down, but a sound, practical teaching and coaching point is to have the hands with the little finger up, or even with the palms facing slightly up. With the arm in this position, the elbow is high and the shoulder joint unlocked, allowing maximum clearance over the water. Further, holding the hands at this angle, is a continuation of the palm or thumb uppermost release described earlier and a preparation for the pitched, soft

entry, elbow high.

Some swimmers fling the arms forward in recovery using much speed and strength. Centripetal force will then straighten the arms, although an acceptable entry is still obtainable. This high speed recovery is sometimes seen in learners and in those with poor buoyancy and shoulder mobility, because for them it is urgent to get their arms forward and into the water as early as possible. The arms provide the main propulsion in butterfly.

Breathing

Breathing is of the explosive type, with leakage of air from the nose and mouth starting underwater as the lungs fill and the muscles

Fig 64   Butterfly arm recovery with the little finger up and the head returning to the water well before the arms.

around the chest work powerfully on the arms. As the mouth clears the water, the neck is extended, the lungs are explosively emptied and immediately refilled. At this point the arms are completing, or have completed, the push phase, which is also the point of maximum acceleration in the stroke cycle. The mouth closes and the head is speedily returned to its normal swimming position, before the arms complete their recovery. The whole breathing movement takes a few tenths of a second and needs powerful muscles of respiration.

The mouth is facing directly forward and teachers and coaches should watch to see that learners, or more experienced swimmers in a demanding session, do not turn the head to one side. A few swimmers have adopted the 'side-breathing' technique, but for most it brings the risk of disturbance of the body position, with an illegal, dropped shoulder, which in turn may cause an asymmetrical arm action, to which the legs will add an irregular balancing kick.

Seen from the side, breathing takes place when the body is fully extended, from nose to toes, and the arms are streamlined close to the side of the body. It is called the canoe position.

Early breathing occurs when the arms are still in their push phase, perhaps only just into it, and the relaxation of the upper body, as the breath is taken, makes a strong push impossible. A firm base is needed for a powerful push. Some swimmers have a very good push on the non-breathing stroke, but a poor one when they are on the breathing cycle, due to early breathing. Teachers and coaches concentrate attention on pushing right through and then breathing.

Beginners might even breathe when the arms are at entry or catch points, using a long arm glide while a much needed breath is taken. This breaks the continuity of the flowing, rhythmic undulation essential to butterfly,

but teachers will show sympathy to learners.

Late breathing describes the badly co-ordinated attempts to breathe as the arms recover over the water, when the down thrust is at its greatest. A swimmer trying to breathe like this will need the help of the teacher.

In a training session, a coach may well observe tiring butterfly swimmers turning the head partly to the side (or further than normal) and will have to decide whether to correct it or accept it as something the swimmer would not do in competition.

Timing

It has already been stated that there are some strong swimmers who have a long push in the arm action and that conversely there are those who have a weak incomplete push, or no push at all. Newton's third law, when applied to swimming, explains the reaction of the feet towards the hands and the reaction of the hips away. If the swimmer has a strong push phase, then the feet and hips will react but, obviously, a weak push evokes a weak re-action and the absence of a push will produce no reaction at all.

Experienced observers of swimmers will recognise the similar body adjustment and foot movement present in a breaststroke start or turn due to the long push through of the hands permitted at that time.

Therefore, in butterfly of good technique, there are two leg kicks to one arm cycle. The first leg kick is to counterbalance the down thrust of the overwater arm recovery, coupled with the down thrust of the head and shoulders on the breathing stroke. This first kick occurs as the head is returned to the water, swiftly followed by the arms.

The second leg kick, if present, occurs at the end of a strong push phase or, should there be an incomplete push, when the hands cease to exert pressure. A descriptive, helpful teaching and coaching point is 'kick the hands in and kick the hands out'.

Many proficient swimmers have the two kicks of similar strength, in which case they are termed *equal beat.* When the second kick is obviously weaker than the first, it is called a *major/minor* kick. Absence of any second kick leads logically to the *single beat.*

The single beat is associated with the vee-pull, to be seen used by learners, by those whose physical build makes it difficult to match the stroke requirements, and by those who are simply not strong enough to complete the arm action.

Discerning teachers and coaches will note that some swimmers will use a 'two beat' kick on the non-breathing cycle, but a 'major/minor' kick on the breathing cycle, often because of breathing too early and not holding the breath until the arm action is completed.

Discussion reveals the opinion of some coaches that there are swimmers who use a 'minor/major' kick. Judgement is reserved on this, until film or photographic records establish the amplitudes of the kicks relative to the swimmer's own body and then to each other, but the following facts favour the opinion. In frontcrawl and backcrawl, the point of maximum acceleration matches the push phase, when the arms are at maximum speed and pitching of the hands employs Bernoulli principles and the arms are also at the point of minimum resistance. A skilled butterfly swimmer is seen to change the pitch of the hands as the long, powerful, accelerating movement from catch to release is made, creating the conditions for a swimmer of high buoyancy and less down thrust problems, to have a stronger second beat.

It is repeated that the timing in butterfly involves the skilled integration of the body position and its movements, of the leg and arm actions and of the breathing.

Butterfly Pre-requisites

1. The ability to open the eyes underwater.
2. Watermanship of a high order.
3. Aquatic breathing.
4. A developed front and backcrawl kick.
5. The ability to swim in straight lines.
6. A streamlined push and glide from the wall.

Teaching Butterfly
(Figs 65 & 66)

It has long been assumed that butterfly should be taught last of the four recognised strokes, but some swimming teachers have discovered that the stroke can be introduced as fun to young beginners. It is possible for children to enjoy short distances swimming their version of the butterfly, provided that the teacher uses common sense and keeps the demand low.

Begin at the rail, with a double leg kick. 'Feet tied together' is a teaching point children grasp readily. Transfer the leg kick to a float, with the child on the front or on the back. The latter is another way of reducing the demand on a learner and progresses to the same action without a supporting float, but with sculling. A parallel progression is the dolphin leg kick with breaststroke arm action, which neatly co-ordinates with a quick lift of the head for breathing. Children also enjoy trying to swim on the side underwater, imitating a fish.

The arm action is taught with the child in shallow water, shoulders under, performing the double, circular arm action, which gives the feeling of the arm movement underwater and of the recovery through the air. Make sure that the arm is long and that the action is not with elbows leading.

For the next progression, it is necessary to arrange the pupil, or pupils according to height, so that the water-line is comfortably at the shoulder. The learner jumps, from both

Butterfly

Fig 65   Beginners try 'kangeroo jumps' as an
introduction to butterfly arm action.

Fig 66   A learner on a drill swimming butterfly
with one arm, buoyancy being
provided by the float. Note the in-
toeing of his feet.

feet, lifting the body a little from the water, and makes the arm action simultaneously with the jump. Following this, the learner adds ducking underwater after the jump so that the arms are down as the head is under, which simulates the feeling of butterfly. The logical progression is to move across the pool, using the double foot jump and the double arm action, at which stage some learners lean forward, which raises the feet, and swim a stroke or two of butterfly. This last progression is known as 'kangaroo jumps'.

With the distances limited, the learner is able to swim short bursts without breathing while the stroke rhythm and coordination develop. A lot of teaching and learning time must be devoted to letting the stroke grow with the use of one arm drills, when the swimmer has one hand grasping the float and the other arm is used in a butterfly action, initially with the head up, or with the body rolled to one side for ease of breathing, but later with the face in the water, lifting for a breath at the correct time. Similar one arm drills can be built around swimming on the back and eventually the front or back drills are repeated, but without a float. A very successful drill is to swim with, say, left arm only, right arm only, both arms together and with a breath.

It helps learners considerably if momentum into the stroke is gained from a vigorous push off the wall or from a plunge dive, when the arm and leg action match the speed of the streamlined body.

Coaching Butterfly

Once the skilled flow and rhythm of butterfly is mastered for short distances of widths or a length, the problem of extending the distance without damaging the skill has to be met.

Over distance, frontcrawl or backcrawl will increase the swimmer's basic fitness, and the vast majority of coaches avoid over distance

butterfly. The preference is to build the strength and endurance required with stroke drills employing single arm actions and using floats, kickboards, flippers and, eventually, hand paddles, with the swimmer on the front and on the back.

Patterned swimming is widely used, and the thinking coach will arrange the drills in order of difficulty, remembering that the order will be different for different swimmers, at different times in the competitive year.

Exercises

1. Swim one arm up the length and the other arm on the way back.
2. Swim two, three or four strokes of one arm and then of the other.
3. Swim three, four or five leg kicks, followed by an arm cycle with breathing.

Drills of this kind can be modified to give a wide range of demands and progressions, and skills can be emphasised by choosing whether to start an arm cycle with the arms extended beyond the head, at the catch point, or at the side ready for release and recovery. If the former is chosen, emphasis can be placed on one aspect of the underwater action and if the latter, stress is put on the recovery action. This is a general principle which coaches utilise to emphasise a selected aspect of skill in strokes with overwater recovery.

Practice

Swimming on the back enables the performer to watch the double leg kick and to check its action, as well as feeling that it involves the hips. The movement is the same when swimming on the front so the body position is checked at the same time.

With the eyes open and looking forward and downward, it is possible to watch the

Butterfly

hands enter the water and to see as well as feel the catch, the outward, downward, backward press of the pull phase, with the elbows high. If the elbows are leading markedly, it is easily seen. Lowering the head a small amount permits watching the arms through their propulsive action, but the recovery will have to be checked by the sense of feel, to find whether the palm or the thumb is down.

When the breath is taken, the thumbs should be able to brush the thighs below the line of the costume and, if this is correct, the timing is most probably correct too.

5 Breaststroke

INTRODUCTION

Breaststroke, in one of its many forms, is the life-saving stroke, because anybody unfortunate enough to fall into water unexpectedly is most unlikely to swim frontcrawl, backcrawl or butterfly to rescue themselves and, if rescuing some other person, the final approach at least should be made on breaststroke in order to have the best view of the position.

Because the limbs remain below the surface, the breaststroke gives maximum flotation, but pays a penalty as the underwater recovery of the arms and legs, after their propulsive actions, causes resistance. It is a go–stop stroke, of which the mechanics were for a long time misunderstood, as it was believed that the squeezing together action of the legs produced forward propulsion. In common with other strokes, too, it was believed that a long, straight arm gave the best leverage, until teachers and coaches carefully examined what the best swimmers were doing and thought about why these techniques were successful.

Swimming law has strict requirements for breaststroke.

1. Part of the head must be above the general level of the water at all times.
2. The limb movements must be under or along the surface.
3. The arm and leg movements respectively, must be simultaneous and symmetrical and movements of the feet up and down are not permitted.
4. The feet must be turned outward in the characteristic position for breaststroke propulsion. It is called dorsi-flexion and the opposite movement, which points the feet and toes as in the crawl strokes, is called plantar flexion.
5. The body must remain on the breast at all times, with the shoulders parallel to the surface of the water and square to the front.

ANALYSIS *(Figs 67 to 73)*

Body Position

The ideal swimming position is a streamlined one, as taken up by good divers. Movements of limbs away from this shape, or deviation of the whole shape, produce resistance.

Breaststroke swimmers must breathe regularly, and the simplest solution is to hold the head out of the water all the time and swim with the body angled downwards to a greater or lesser degree. Recreational swimmers and learners choose this position, as the face is clear of the water, giving easy breathing and clear vision. The resistance factor is unimportant because these swimmers have little interest in speed. Resistance is largely a problem which comes with speed, so the adoption of an angled body position, permanently deviating from the ideal, does not matter to recreational swimmers. It is described as swimming with a fixed head position.

The ideal swimming position is also often described as being flat and streamlined. If a breaststroker tries to be flat, with the hips well up as in the frontcrawl, then the feet would break the surface, which contravenes swim-

Breaststroke

Fig 67 The arms are nearly fully recovered and the feet are about to turn outwards. Notice that the crown of the head is above the surface, and observe too the angle between the trunk and the thighs.

Fig 69 The heels are making a curved pathway as they accelerate out and round. The arms remain fully extended.

Fig 68 A medium width whip kick is likely to follow a medium shaped W. The feet are now fully everted, and the arms fully extended.

Fig 70 The hips remain high and steady throughout the stroke – compare them with the line on the wall.

Fig 71 As the feet whip together, the arms are ready to start their pull.

Fig 72 The arms pull until level with the shoulders and the hands start to change pitch as they swirl inwards. Note that the head is clear of the water for late breathing.

Fig 73 The hands, without pausing, turn palms up ready for recovery. The elbows tuck in for streamlining and the feet are pointed for the same reason.

ming law. Should the breaststroker decide to submerge the body completely, in order to keep the feet underwater, then the head could well be underwater also, in contravention of swimming law. Various compromises are to be seen as solutions to this dilemma.

There are some swimmers who hold the head up and angle the hips to keep the feet under and, as the strong, propulsive kick is made, they lower the head into the water, carefully keeping part of it above water. For part of the stroke cycle, it allows a streamlined position, which is often held as a glide, giving economical swimming. Those with high buoyancy are able to use this kind of technique, and sinkers might just have a brief glide. The movement of lowering the head is at times exaggerated or over-vigorous and gives rise to an ungainly rocking body movement.

Another solution to the dilemma has been developed by top class breaststroke swimmers and comprises swimming with the hips in a fixed position, safely below the surface so

Breaststroke

that the leg action is legal, while a part of the head is legally showing above the surface. This creates a body position for a powerful leg action, kicking directly backwards, without a large wasteful component angled downwards. The breathing takes place with a lift of the head and shoulders, sufficient to have the mouth clear the large wave pushed up by the raised upper body. Breath must be taken very quickly and the head and shoulders lowered at once to remove the high resistance. It is a compromise and the powerful leg action is strong enough to compensate amply for the resistance.

Young swimmers and their instructors are as prone to follow new styles as people everywhere, and the raising of the head and shoulders for breathing is to be seen exaggerated, as is the fast return of the head and shoulders to the water, with a movement similar to one in dolphin butterfly. Teachers and coaches will wisely have their swimmers try all techniques and settle on that which best matches the individual.

Leg Action

There are two distinct leg actions, and study of old printed and photographic material relevant to breaststroke shows that during the period when one action was being exclusively taught, the second and better kick was used by swimmers to whom it came quite naturally.

The Wedge Kick (Fig 74)

The wedge kick has been taught for many years, and was based on spreading the legs and squeezing away the wedge of water they held between them, by closing the gap. Trials with straight legs, while ensuring that there is no ankle movement; show this to be impossible, for movement derives from bending and straightening a limb. It also puts the legs in a

position of great resistance. This having been stated, it must be recognised that there are swimmers who, for a number of physical reasons, are happy with the wedge kick, which is sufficient for recreation.

Seen from the side, the legs are recovered from the stretched glide position, being brought forward and flexed until there is either a right angle at the hip, with the thighs pointing straight down, knees flexed, or with the knees brought further forward of this position, so that the thighs are pointing forward and downward. It is a high resistance position and the further forward the knees are carried, the higher the drag.

In breaststroke, the leg is the lever, and it is the inside of the foot which becomes the paddle when dorsi-flexed. The recovered position described in the previous paragraph places the foot so that at worst the sole is facing backwards and at best, partly backwards, which gives the instep an impossible or poor position for thrust.

From this position the legs are straightened, often as wide as possible, the actual angle depending on personal hip mobility. The soles of the feet press on the water, or only part of the instep presses, usually late in the leg extension. Resistance comes from the wide spread of the legs, and it decreases as the legs close to hip width or inside it. This is referred to as being inside the body's shadow or silhouette, which implies a low resistance. It is late in the leg action when there is sufficient propulsion to overcome the high resistance.

Viewed from the rear, the recovered position shows that often the heels are touching and that the knees are spread much wider than the width of the hips. The soles of the feet face backwards, or partly so, depending on the knee and hip relationship. As the legs extend, they straighten while remaining outside the width of the hips, which leaves no further contribution to be made to propulsion,

56

Fig 74 Wedge kick. The knees are fully extended wide of the hips and the soles of the feet facing backwards, with no more thrust to give, but much resistance to overcome.

but an addition to resistance instead. The legs squeeze together and the heels touch with the toes pointed, many swimmers having been taught to complete the leg action by bringing the heels together. There is small acceleration of the feet during the wedge kick.

The Whip Kick (Fig 75)

The whip kick is mechanically more efficient than the wedge. Viewed from the side, the knees are well behind a vertical line descending from the hip, which gives a smoother water flow, lessening the resistance. The inside surface of the foot faces backward, where it can gain maximum purchase on the water, the equivalent of a good catch point for the hands. This comparison with the hands is one which is very descriptive of outstanding breaststrokers, who appear to possess in the feet a feel and sensitivity normally associated with supple hands. From the recovered position, the legs extend backwards and there is often a weak downward component.

When viewed from the rear, the recovered positions of whip kick breaststroke show a range of attitudes deriving from individual characteristics. The teacher or coach will look at the distance between the heels and between the knees. When seen like this and associated with the individual hip width of the swimmer, the three widths, feet, hips, knees, may be generalised as a capital W. The 'breaststroke W', as it is called, varies considerably, some being tall and narrow and others being wider, either at the top or the

Fig 75 Whip kick. High hip position and heels close to the seat. The knees could be closer together, but the soles are facing upwards and the knees behind the hips.

bottom.

From the W position adopted, the legs kick back in an accelerating movement, the heels leading in a path which moves out and then in, thus creating a curved limb track, better seen from directly overhead. The radius of the curve will depend on the individual physical build of the swimmer, but the end result is that the legs straighten only when behind the hips, inside the body shadow, so that propulsion is gained all the way and resistance minimised. The accelerating movement is often continued by expert, natural swimmers, so that it ends with the big toes touching due to strong inward rotation of the legs, combining with the speed attained to give a propeller action as the feet change from a dorsi-flexed position to an extended streamlined one. The swirl of the feet in this action is strongly reminiscent of the pitching of the hands in sculling.

Arm Action

Most breaststroke swimmers gain the larger part of their propulsion from the leg action, although there are some whose arm and leg actions contribute approximately half each, and there are a few whose physical build gives them an arm action which dominates the stroke.

Swimming law requires the limb movements to be under the water, and consequently analysis of breaststroke excludes entry. There must be discussion of the arms and hands in the glide position, where they are extended forward, often with the palms down and the thumbs touching, in a streamlined position. Care must be taken to avoid excessive extension of the shoulder, which may so place the joint that the muscle action is weakened.

Another arm and hand position frequently met is with the thumbs touching and with the little fingers raised, so that the palms are facing both outward and downward. The inward rotation of the arm which achieves this, is analogous to the soft, pitched entry used in the other three strokes, in that the elbow is raised and thus prepared for high elbow arm action. When the palm down position described in the previous paragraph is used, the elbows are underneath the arm and liable to lead the action. Elbow leading movements are propulsively weak, though suited to many learners and to recreational swimmers.

Catch Point

In the other three recognised strokes, the catch is some few inches below the surface, usually six to eight inches (15–20 cm). In these strokes, following entry, the hand or hands move immediately to catch point. In breaststroke, many swimmers are taught to push the hands forward, just below the surface, where they are frequently held in a glide action. Close observation shows that swimmers may have a shorter or longer arm glide coupled with a leg glide, but there are those who have an arm glide and no leg glide. The opposite is also to be found.

If the hands are pushed forward together in a shallow action, with or without a subsequent glide, there is a delayed downward and outward movement to catch point. A coaching instruction to swimmers sometimes heard, is for the hands to be pushed forward and, as the arms extend, for the hands then to be pushed downward in an action reminiscent of the early press upon the water found in good

crawl and butterfly swimming. It avoids the brief delay.

Swimmers using the palm downward starting position tend to drift the hands apart and downward which is acceptable for leisurely swimming. Competitive swimmers need the early catch point, with the hands and arms shaped for the succeeding pull phase.

Pull Phase – Straight Arm Action (Fig 76)

A straight arm action must involve some degree of elbow flexion and extension, but it is a descriptive title, as the arms show little flexion. From the catch, the arms pull sideways and downwards, the depth of the pull depending on several factors. Beginners may well press down considerably, because reaction will lift the head and shoulders. Recreational swimmers of high buoyancy, with no difficulty in keeping the face clear of the water, may well pull mainly sideways. The straight arm pull usually ends with each arm held at 45 degrees outwards and 45 degrees downwards from the centre line, but obviously some have a narrower or wider action to meet personal physical build. The fingertips are normally just at the edge of the field of vision, when the eyes are looking straight ahead.

If the wider action is used, there are some who pull until the arms are stretched out sideways, level with or even beyond the shoulders. This is an error, even though the performer may enjoy the feeling of using strength, because the action leaves the arms in a high resistance position and one from which further resistance will be created as the arms are recovered for the next stroke.

Recovery is effected by bending the elbows, while moving the hands inwards. Several common errors occur at this stage.

As the hands come together, the elbows are held in a fixed position, which gives high

Breaststroke

resistance. If the hands are slid palms downwards towards each other until the thumbs touch, it adds to the tendency to hold the elbows out. It helps if the palms face each other, or at least face partly inwards, as this streamlines the elbow position.

Some learners are taught, by word and by demonstration, to recover the hands in a position close under the chin. The action, for a person in a prone position in water and not standing upright on the poolside, is actually deeper, at approximately the same depth as the elbows, or a little above them. From this point, the hands are pushed forward until ready to start the sequence again.

Pull Phase – Bent Arm Action (Fig 77)

The hands are pressed downwards, sideways and backwards, initially with the palms facing partly outwards, but changing pitch through the movement until they are facing backwards. Flexion of the elbow accompanies the movement, but the elbow is kept high. It is an accelerating movement, reaching a position where the elbows are wide of the shoulders, below them. The hands are usually wide of the elbows, but some swimmers have them at the same width or inside it, in order to shorten the lever. The effective length of the lever is a line from the pivot point in the shoulder to the hand.

Fig 76 A wide straight arm pull and an exaggerated head down position forces the seat out of the water. Later it will be a useful way to start a head first surface dive.

The arm pull should end when level with the shoulders, as stated above, and there can be no push phase, in the sense of the long push through used in the other three strokes. However, some experienced teachers and coaches argue that the next movement is a push and describe it as such.

During the last stages of the pull and as a smooth, accelerating continuation of it, the elbows begin to bend and the hands move rapidly together. As they do so, the hands change pitch so that from facing backwards, fingertips down, they end with the palms facing each other, fingertips pointing forward. The movement is aptly described as a swirl, and it is a powerful sculling action, the speed of which combines with the hands' pitch

changes to use Bernoulli principles to gain thrust.

Some swimmers continue the pitch changing of the hands by rotating the arms outwards until the palms are facing partly or directly upwards. Such rotation may be classed as one of the exaggerated movements mentioned several times earlier, but it has the beneficial effect of streamlining the elbows, in an action described as 'shutting the elbows'.

Breathing

For the leisure swimmer, breathing brings no difficulty, as the face is clear of the water, or a small movement makes it so. Those swimming with a fixed head position and learners,

Fig 77 Bent arm action – the upper arm in position for a powerful pull using the muscles around the shoulder to best advantage. The palms face the rear and the hands, elbows and shoulders are all in line.

will almost certainly breathe when the arms are extended forward, or moving forward to that position. Often the breath is taken at the same time as a glide, whether a full glide or a partial one.

The slow long arm action lends itself to slow breathing, and the lungs empty and refill with an easy trickling in and out of air. Bubbles show that air is leaking from the mouth underwater, but the great part of exhalation happens with the mouth above water, to be followed at once by inhalation. Breath is taken once every stroke cycle.

The bent arm action, with a whip kick, used by competitive swimmers, employs fast movements of the limbs and the head is partly submerged with the fixed hip body position. Raising the head and shoulders at racing speeds raises a large wave directly in front of the swimmer. In consequence of these factors, explosive breathing is used. Some air is exhaled underwater, but the powerful exhalation is largely completed as the chin is pushed forward and the mouth is clear of the water. On the rebound of the powerful use of respiratory muscles, inhalation occurs, and the head and shoulders return quickly to a more streamlined position. Most competitive swimmers breathe every stroke cycle, although breath holding to retain a streamlined position might be used at the end of a race with a close finish.

Timing

The long arm breaststroke swimmer takes breath at the non-propulsive stage of the stroke cycle and also at the point of maximum acceleration. Leg action is the main propulsive force in breaststroke, and the body moves forward as the legs finish their kick, at which time the arms are being extended forward. Exhalation takes place at this time and is called early breathing. Many thousands of children have been taught with the instruction to 'blow their fingers forward', which leads at once to early breathing. Slight variations exist as the precise moment of breathing, but the arms are well forward.

The timing fits to the rhythm of arm pull; leg kick; breathe; arm pull; leg kick; breathe. Or arm pull; leg kick; breathe and glide and repeat. It can be thought of as 'breathing off the legs', a descriptive phrase.

Bent arm breaststroke, with its whip kick and explosive breathing, has a radically different timing, but it obeys the rules of breathing at a non-propulsive stage and when the body has its highest speed. Directly the arms and hands have completed the swirling action, the head and shoulders are raised for the breath and then returned to the water, as the powerful whip kick is executed and the arms are extended forward.

The rhythm of the timing is: (arm) pull; breathe; kick; pull; breathe; kick. Sometimes there is a slight pause following the arm pull and the rhythm could be written: pull; breathe . . .; kick; pull; breathe . . .; kick.

Because of the vast range of build, age, strength and flexibility found among swimmers, there will exist a parallel range of timings, with those above as the extremes. One example is termed 'mid-way breathing' in breaststroke, and needs little explanation, beyond saying that the arms are half-way through the pull action.

In an earlier section, attention was drawn to the necessity of breath holding during physical exercise. No breath should be taken until the arms have completed their movements, because the muscles moving the arms are grouped around the chest wall, so that the relaxation of the chest wall concomitant with breathing reduces the effectiveness of the arm action, even to the point of stopping it completely. It follows that, normally, breathing is best left until the arms have finished their task, but in breaststroke it is possible to breathe at any point in the arm action. The teacher will notice that those swimmers with stronger arms will pull perhaps a third, a half, or two-thirds of the way through the possible full arm movement and then take breath. Also, the teacher will notice some swimmers with weaker arms who use just a small hand movement and then take breath, so that they are virtually swimming with the legs only.

Breaststroke Pre-requisites

There are none. The most important decision is to use the multi-stroke method of teaching and watch for those who are natural breast-strokers.

Teaching Breaststroke
(Figs 78 to 80)

Human beings can be grouped in many ways: some are tall and some are short; some are thin and some are fat; there are women and there are men. They also are found to be naturally symmetrical or naturally alternating in limb movements, and therefore take naturally to breaststroke, or otherwise.

In the crawl type strokes, the water pressure is sensed by the nerve endings present on the top of the foot. Breaststroke, with its dorsi-flexed foot position, requires that the water pressure is sensed by nerve endings situated on the inner surfaces of the foot.

Once a swimmer has found how to gain propulsion, with either the top of the foot, or

Fig 78   Breaststroke arm action, copying the teacher's demonstration.

Breaststroke

Fig 79 A learner using floats shows one knee pointing down and the sole of the foot pointing mainly upwards on one leg, while the other leg has its knee pointing outwards and the sole facing backwards. The left leg is ready for a whip kick, but the right is prepared for a wedge.

with its inside surface, there is often impedance to learning the other one. The arm action prompts little difficulty, but a simultaneous and symmetrical leg action does. It must be accepted that, due to the importance it holds as a life-saving stroke, some form of breaststroke, even if it infringes swimming law, must be taught and practised. A teacher will take pains, though, to correct what is legally wrong. It is the feet and the legs which cause difficulty.

If taught as a first stroke, as it was for many years, the breaststroke normally takes much longer than dog-paddle, for example, before the learners are swimming. It is a common

teaching experience to have non-swimmers off on dog-paddle during the first or second lesson. Breaststroke takes longer, but once the swimmer has the basic skill, progress is very rapid and in a matter of weeks or months, the swimmer will be achieving long distances. Conversely, the dog-paddle swimmer with a very early start, will then usually take months before the basic skill is absorbed and longer still to achieve distances. The importance of multi-stroke teaching and of developing that stroke most natural to the individual is obvious.

Begin at the rail and transfer the skill to the float, but keep to short distances or even to a

Fig 80   *A learner kicks with pointed toes.*

limited number of leg kicks. Often a tidy leg kick deteriorates because the learner has been instructed to swim a width, when two or three kicks only were possible. Demonstrations are more valuable than words.

The arm action is usually easily grasped and practised, in shallow water. Arms only, with the legs isolated and immobile, is too difficult for beginners and improvers. Leave it out. Put the arm and leg actions together for a few strokes only, while learning takes place.

Swimming on the back, with life-saving leg kick, uses actions relevant to breaststroke. It allows the swimmer to use the eyes to check the leg action and foot position.

Breaststrokers will spend a lot of time kicking with a float or board, in order to develop a smooth, tireless leg action. Look for the incorrect leg action which combines a whip kick one leg and a wedge kick with the other, then correct the offending knee.

Remember that youngsters might feel needlessly guilty for having an illegal stroke when there is not the remotest chance that competition will involve them. Life-saving comes before laws.

Coaching Breaststroke

Over-distance breaststroke is not used by coaches and the stroke is unsuited as a warm-up, because of the possible stress to the knees. Breaststroke, on the front or back, is useful for a swim-down, if used, at the conclusion of a hard work-out.

Breaststrokers, unlike frontcrawlers, appear to mature very rapidly and spring to the fore quickly in the particular level of competition involved. Watch for them.

Because it is the slowest stroke, breaststroke swimmers often suffer by being always last in the lane, last to finish a set of swims and nearly always being in another swimmer's wake. Lane and pool organisation should recognise the needs of all the swimmers.

The timing in breaststroke is critical and, where it is possible to get by with strength and endurance in the other three strokes, it is not so with breaststroke. A change in timing could be the cause of a large drop in performance.

Medley swimming is excellent for conditioning and involves all the swimmers with breaststroke, as well as all the breaststrokers with the other strokes. Flexibility is as important for breaststroke as it is for the other strokes.

Practice

A pair of goggles allow the face to be dipped into the water where an accurate check on the arm action can be made. A careful look at which way the palms face is important.

Fortunately the leg action on the front and on the back are similar, so if one is symmetrical, then the other is as well. Swimming on the back with the head raised, possibly with the aid of floats, permits the action of the legs to be seen.

A check on whether the face is clear of the water, partly submerged, or nearly fully submerged, will indicate the type of body position.

The time at which breath is taken can be tested by abruptly stopping swimming when breathing out and noting the position of the arms.

6 Diving, Dive Starts and Finishes

INTRODUCTION

The common factors in diving, starts and turns, are the ability to jump, which is based on the use of middle and outer range activity of a joint, and transfer of momentum.

Transfer of Momentum

Transfer of momentum occurs when something is moving and then stops, and the energy of the movement is passed on. A snooker player uses the energy of the cue ball to pot another ball. A car rolling gently down a slope into another car will jolt it forward. An arm swinging powerfully and suddenly stopping, will transfer its energy to the body on which it swings, and this is why people swing their arms in trying to jump up high, or swimmers in trying to 'jump' outwards in a racing dive. Transfer of momentum will happen only if the diver's feet are in contact with the ground. Once the feet are off the ground, the centre of gravity of the diver or jumper will follow a path pre-determined by the force of the jump and the angle of take-off.

Ranges of Movement *(Fig 81)*

The arm has a range of movement from fully extended, or straight, to fully flexed, or bent. From the fully flexed position, the first third of movement is called inner range, the second third middle range and the last third outer range.

Unless special training is undertaken, the inner range of movement is weak. People who do train to develop strength of the inner range are boxers, who train to have a powerful short arm jab, and weight lifters, who need to move massive weights through the inner range on the way to a lift. For most people, though, this position is weak and movement through it tends to be slow.

The middle range is usually the strong part of the movement, because it is where most exercise of the joint and its associated muscles happens. Rugby players in a scrum prepare to push their opponents off the ball by placing the knees and hips in a middle range position. On the running track, a sprinter getting on his starting blocks is placing himself in the ideal middle range position of one leg for a thrust forward. A swimmer in a racing start bends at the hip and knee into a middle range position for maximum strength applied to a fast start.

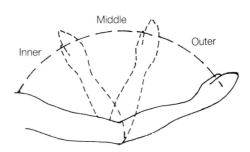

Fig 81   Inner, middle and outer ranges of movement.

Outer range movement is fast movement, if it receives acceleration from the middle range initially, or if special training through that range is undertaken. Many swimmers performing a racing turn adjust the body to a middle range position at knee and hip for a powerful push off, starting at the hip and ending with the smaller muscles which finally extend the toes, but each joint will have passed through middle and outer range in succession. There are swimmers, strong enough and sufficiently skilled, who place the body in outer range position for the turn and then generate all the speed required through the outer range alone.

LEARNING TO DIVE *(Fig 82)*

Diving, the skill of leaping and jumping, begins in shallow water. Learners jumping up and down are feeling the extension or straightening of the whole body which occurs in diving, and they add the swing of the arms with an extension over the head quite naturally, at times.

The ideal diving position is the ideal swimming position, with the hands streamlined, the arms pressed against the head, the body held firmly in a straight line and the legs pressed together with the toes pointed. The head should be held in a natural position in line with the body.

This position is demonstrated and taught and the learners try to achieve it in the water, jumping from the bottom. A more strenuous exercise is to pair off and for one partner to hold the arm along the surface of the water while the other attempts to clear it with a dive which requires a strong push off the bottom. Plastic hoops of the appropriate size may be used, if available. Another partner activity is to push from the bottom, to pass through the other's straddled legs. Handstands also teach the required position, as does any activity which has the body in a controlled stretch from fingers to toes. All these lead to the push and glide from the side wall of the pool.

Checkpoints

Two teaching and coaching points need to be mentioned:

1. The hands should be placed one on top of the other for maximum streamlining.
2. The body should be held in a firm, straight position, as described above, until it surfaces after the push and glide. Many swimmers relax the body after the initial push and lose the fine edge of streamlining.

Both of these points should become natural to the swimmers from an early stage.

Jumping from the Side *(Fig 83)*

Parallel with the push and glide activities in the water, jumping from the side commences, with caution and safety, as children approach it usually with excitement. Jumping in for the timid may need an assistant in the water and use of the steps to reduce the drop into the water.

Jumps start with toes over the edge for a safe grip and the body upright, arms at the side. A step into the water is made and the foot remaining on the side, having given support for the step, joins the other leg for double footed entry. As confidence grows, the step becomes an upward leap, however modest, combined with an upward swing of the arms, to achieve the feet first entry in the streamlined position. This progresses to a double foot take-off, which is more difficult to control and should be performed gently at first.

Fig 82   Diving begins in the water.

Fig 83   Jumping in is great fun and the water is safely clear of swimmers in this area.

Variations

Once the double foot take-off jump is mastered, variations are introduced, always with caution and safety.

1. Jump in sideways.
2. Jump in backwards.
3. Jump in with a quarter twist, a half twist, a threequarter twist and full twist. (A very strong jump is needed to achieve more than a full twist.)
4. Jump in with a rapid bend of the knees to a tuck position and then straighten for entry.
5. Jump in, make a star shape and straighten for entry.
6. Jump in, make a pike shape and hold it to enter hips first.

While the jumping practices listed are being taught, diving is also developing from the side.

69

Diving, Dive Starts and Finishes

A series of tried and trusted progressions are used, but no one should move on until competent at the level in use.

Sitting Dive *(Figs 84 & 85)*

The feet are placed side by side or up to hip width apart in the trough or on the rail, should there be one. In deck level pools, steps may be used; otherwise this practice must be omitted. The knees may be placed apart for very timid children, but normally they will be together or only a little apart. The back is rounded so that the top of the head is pointed at the water, with the arms pressed against the ears and one hand on top of the other. The seat should not be far back, but should be close enough to the edge to permit the body to fall forward.

Fig 84 A sitting dive, with the feet firmly in the trough to provide a sound base for thrust. The head is nicely down and the arms are tight against the ears.

First attempts may have the timid diver entering the water by passing the body between the spread knees. Others will lift the hips in falling forward before extending the body and pushing with the feet. At this stage, the instruction must always be for the diver to 'go for distance', to avoid attempts at a more vertical entry.

Kneeling Dive

From the sitting dive, with a clear lift of the hips, progression is made to the kneeling dive. The toes of one foot grip the edge, while the knee of the other is placed alongside that foot and the body, head and arms pointed at the water. The hips are raised as the body rocks forward over the foot gripping the edge and the body is extended as the leg straightens. Both legs come together before entry. The basic instruction is 'go for distance'.

For the two progressive practices above, the teacher should check that the head is held down between the arms. Raising the head with a belly-flop entry is caused by fear. If it happens, revert to diving practices in shallow water until the correct position is achieved.

Lunge Dive *(Figs 86 & 87)*

Teachers sometimes omit the kneeling dive, to go straight to the lunge dive. When the body is raised from the kneeling position, it takes up the lunge position, with the weight on the leading foot. The rear foot can supply the small push needed to overbalance the body and the leading foot supplies the thrust away from the edge. The legs join and a streamlined body 'goes for distance'.

Standing Dive

Next is the standing dive, where the learner has both feet gripping the edge, hip width

Fig 85   Lift the hips and push. The arms are
streamlined against the head.

apart, and the body is bent at the knee and
hip, with the upper body, head and arms
curved and pointed at the water. The amount
of bend at the knee and hip will indicate the
degree of confidence the performer has. The
arms are held still and the body falls forward,
for the hips and knees to straighten to give a
streamlined entry, going for distance.

Pike Fall

Last in this series of progressions is the pike
fall. Both feet grip the edge and for first
attempts, the feet and legs may be apart to
provide a more secure balance. Later they will
be side by side. The hips are deeply bent, in a
bowing position, but the back should be
straight with the head in line. The arms form a
capital Y shape and are held in the same plane

as the body.

The knees rapidly bend and straighten for a
vigorous thrust as the body overbalances.
The arms are brought to the position already
taught, alongside the head during the flight,
which will be higher than hitherto and,
although the diver will still be aiming for distance with a streamlined body position, the
depth after entry will be greater.

Watching the feet of divers will repay the
teacher, as the feet should extend powerfully
when they leave the edge and they should
stay streamlined during the flight, the entry
and the underwater glide. If the feet do not
extend, the swimmer is not obtaining maximum thrust and maximum streamlining.

Before separating the diving paths available
to the learner at this stage, it must be stated
that a good teacher will always remember that

Fig 86 The lunge dive showing the thrust
from the standing leg and the
extension of the body. This learner
shows a good head position and has
learned very early to place one hand
on top of the other.

Fig 87 A nearly fully extended lunge dive. The
diver's legs are ready to join together.

diving is based on the jumping ability. Should children have low jumping abilities, a long dive ootwards or a high take-off upwards will be impossible for them, but they should still learn to streamline well and make the best of what they are able to do.

ANALYSIS

Analysis of dives is made under the following headings:

1. Stance – the position taken prior to the starting signal.
2. Drop – the movements made after the starting signal to get the body into position for the drive.
3. Drive or take-off – the extension of the body, the angle of the drive and the transfer of momentum of the arms.
4. Flight – the shape taken by the body in the air.
5. Entry – the shape of the body as it passes into the water.
6. Glide – the length of the glide and the streamlining of the body.
7. Transition – the movements made to bring the body to the surface and into the stroke.

RACING DIVE

Stance

The feet, hip width apart, grip the edge with the toes. The knees are comfortably bent, the hip flexed, and the back held in the natural curve of the spine. The neck follows the natural curve, and the head is held with the eyes looking straight down into the water. The weight is forward, on the balls of the feet.

For a plunge dive, the arms hang loosely down from the shoulders, but for a racing dive, they are held approximately shoulder width apart pointing midway forward and midway downward, usually with the palms facing largely to the water.

Drop

The weight moves back and then forward in movement which is sometimes just a slight rocking motion and sometimes a marked shift which lifts the toes. The arms swing in a large circle, gaining energy. The body drops forward, accelerating by shortening, until it is poised on the edge with approximately 90 degree bend at the knee and hip, in a position for a powerful thrust outwards and upwards. The head is down at this stage.

Drive

A powerful extension of the whole body is made, beginning with the hip, passing to the knee, and finally the feet extend to add to the total. The arms, before the feet break contact, stop in mid-swing, usually pointing somewhere between straight down from the shoulder to a position half-way from straight down to straight ahead. The head is lifted at this point.

Flight

Full extension of the body is held and the hands move forward and together for streamlining as the head is lowered, a movement which causes the body to pike slightly and change direction, pointing downwards to the water.

Entry

The fingertips enter first, and the angle of entry depends on the angle of take-off and the degree of piking in flight. The streamlined arms and body enter the water followed by the legs and pointed feet.

Glide

The length, depth and speed of the glide will depend on the stroke to be swum, the speed of the individual swimmer in that stroke and the skill and power of the individual's start. The depth is controlled by raising or lowering the head.

Transition

As the speed of the glide decreases to a point where no advantage lies in continuing it, the head rises and combines with natural buoyancy and the first limb movements to lift the body to the surface in a swimming position, where the limb movements already started, continue smoothly without pause at race

speed.

There are variations for each of the headings used, which are now listed, with comments.

STARTS

Stance

The Grab Start (Figs 88 & 89)

Hip flexion allows the swimmer to reach down and grip the edge of the starting block, either between or outside the feet. For a start from the edge of the pool, where no grip is possible, the hands press back against the sides. Flexibility is required for the position, and those lacking it tend to acquire an ungainly crouch. Probably such people would be better adopting another technique.

Fig 88 The stance for the grab start with hands outside the feet and eyes looking straight down.

Fig 89 Alternative stance for the grab start showing hands between the feet and eyes looking back.

The body weight is well forward, ready to overbalance immediately, but many young swimmers, from the grab start position, actually circle the arms and use the plunge dive.

Track Start (Fig 90)

One foot is over the edge of the starting block and the other back, as on the running track. Both hands grip the front edge of the block and the weight is back, hanging on the arms which are pulling strongly. The head is looking mainly downward.

Arm up Start (Fig 91)

A variation of the track start is with the arm opposite the forward foot swung back and held raised in the air, while the other hand

Fig 91   The arm-up track start stance.

grips the front of the block. It is for swimmers with strong arms and is borrowed directly from track athletes.

Drop

Grab Start (Fig 92)

If the hands are able to grip the block, a strong pull downwards is made to overbalance the body, which already has its weight well forward, after which the arms swing forward. Teachers and coaches will observe those who, at the starting signal, lift the hands up and then move them forward, showing no pull down against the grip, or press back against the wall, if a grip is not possible. The body drops into the position with the knees and hips flexed for a powerful extension.

Fig 90   Track start position, with the weight back, tensing the arms.

Fig 92 From the grab start, the body drops
        forward, flexing at the knee and the
        hip, which shortens the length of the
        lever, giving faster rotation
        downwards, into a position where the
        hips and knees can extend powerfully.

Track Start

The arms, with the body weight already against them, pull forward at the start signal and, as the body overbalances, continue with a forward swing. Simultaneously the back leg drives the body forward.

If the 'arm up' stance is used, the hand gripping the edge pulls the body forward and downward, aided by the drive of the trailing leg. At the same time, the arm held in the air swings powerfully forward and downward.

In the track start, the arms or arm aid a leg in getting the body overbalanced and moving as fast as possible. It leaves the swimmer with one leg flexed at hip and knee for the drive. The raised arm is timed to join the other arm so that they swing forward together.

Drive *(Figs 93 & 94)*

Grab Start

The main advantage of the grab start over the plunge is the saving of time in overbalancing the body and getting it dropping rapidly into position for the drive. Thereafter the extension of the body is similar in both.

Track Start

The body and the forward leg extend powerfully while the trailing leg is pulled forward with the total body action contributing nothing to the drive. The arms in the arm up version are fully synchronised and swinging forward together.

Fig 93   The feet are just in contact with the
          side and the arms have stopped,
          giving transfer of momentum.

Fig 94   The drive, or take-off. The body is fully
          extended and the extension of the feet
          shows a really hard effort. The arms
          have halted pointing downwards in
          the ideal position for transfer of
          momentum.

Flight

The plunge and grab start are similar at this stage, and the track starts have the legs together and streamlined. Transfer of momentum is the same in all cases.

The piked position necessary to change the body's direction is often very marked following a powerful take-off which is angled upwards. A very flat entry would result without the piking, which is identified by the legs which are horizontal and parallel to the water. It is the body, head and arms which are angled downwards.

During flight, some swimmers very swiftly bend the lower leg, flicking the heels towards the seat and equally rapidly flicking them back again. It is named the 'hitch-kick', a term borrowed from long jump in athletics. The swimmers using it best tend to be breaststrokers who have a long deep underwater glide at the start, so that there is need of an angled take-off and a high flight to give the energy for the glide. Normally the drop of the head in flight is sufficient to provide the body with rotation to make it ready for entry, but with these swimmers, extra rotation is provided by the hitch-kick to steepen the angle of dive.

The angled take-off with high flight, and the subsequent steep angle of entry, have all combined into a very skilled racing dive which is better thought of as a series of curves. The first is a high, curving take-off, followed and matched by a steep, curving angle downwards to the surface.

Entry *(Fig 95)*

The pike dive and the curved dive, which has an American name of 'bubble entry', are both high energy dives, with the energy converting to speed, depth, or both, underwater. The great skill comes at entry, where the body up to the hips is held by the water and the legs, which were parallel to the water, or lower than the line of the body, now move into line with the upper body, driving it down at an angle of 45 degrees. Underwater, particularly in shallow water, the upper body forms another curve as the arms, head and chest are raised until they are parallel with the surface. The rest of the body, the hips and legs, follow the same curve and then straighten. It is a skilled complex movement, akin to a difficult gymnastic feat, and needs expert coaching. Past experience with fashions in swimming dictate caution from teachers and coaches, and watching for unprepared swimmers attempting this dive, especially into shallow water.

Glide

In front and backcrawl and in butterfly, depending on the speed and distance of the race, the glide might be extended by kicking. At sprint distances, with top class swimmers, there is little advantage in extending the glide.

Breaststrokers are permitted one arm pull and one leg kick before surfacing. A sequence of actions for a breaststroke glide would be:

1. *Dive and glide.* Hold the glide.
2. *Arm pull.* The arms pull either right round the side of the body, underneath the body like a butterfly arm action, or somewhere between. Some swimmers use a cross-over position of the hands in the underwater pull and push.
3. *Hold the glide.* The head is lowered at this stage to keep the body at the depth required. The arms are tightly streamlined, palms facing the surface.
4. *Leg recovery and arm recovery.* The arms recover, keeping close to the body to minimise resistance. As the arms extend forward of the shoulders, the leg kick drives the body forward and the head is raised so that the

Fig 95   Pike entry, showing the legs parallel to
the surface of the water, while the
angled body cuts the water. Later the
legs will swing upwards to be in line
with the body. A close look will show
the head well dropped, most probably
to stop the force of the water pulling
the goggles off the face.

body rises to the surface in the racing position. As the head breaks surface, the legs are fully extended as are the arms, ready to move into full stroke.

Transition

The specific aim is to have the body break the surface in a swimming position, with the arms and legs continuing without pause the propulsive movements started at the end of the glide, including the first overwater recovery of the arm, or arms.

THE PLAIN HEADER

The pike fall leads to a dive which is able to take either of two paths and the plunging racing dives, aimed at a shallow entry gaining distance has been described. Should the diver aim for height, the second path is taken, and it leads to the plain header, known to earlier generations as the English header. Some teachers prefer to introduce the plunge before the pike fall. It is a matter of choice.

Diving, Dive Starts and Finishes

Stance *(Figs 96 & 97)*

For the stance, or the ready position, the toes grip the edge of the pool firmly, feet and legs together and the whole body is upright, with the arms held mid-way upwards and outwards, palms of the hands facing forward. It helps hold the body in this upright position if the head is tilted slightly back, by having the eyes look somewhat above their own level. A useful teaching point is to have the diver fix his eyes on a mark or object that creates the position required.

When viewed from the rear, the position is a capital Y and from the side, it is an upright, firm line, but not a rigid one.

Take-off *(Figs 98 & 99)*

The knees bend and, at the same time, the upper body leans forward to a shallow piked shape, which transfers the body weight to the balls of the feet and lifts the heels. At this critical point in the dive, the hips remain vertically above the point of balance, so that the subsequent very rapid extension of the knees and feet sends their thrust through the hips.

Flight *(Figs 100 & 101)*

The slight angle at the hips is held, which creates rotation, turning the body upside down for a head first entry. At take-off and in the first half of the flight, the arms remain in the same position. They should not move forward. In the latter part of the flight they move inwards to close on the head, so that the hands are either side by side, or one hand is pressed on top of the other, stretched and in line with the body, which, in the last stage, straightens for entry. It is a streamlined shape, stretched from fingers to toes.

Fig 96   The ready position from the side.

Fig 97   The ready position from the rear.

Fig 98   Heels raised, hips and weight over the feet, piking at the hip, in a take-off.

Fig 100   Rotation raises the feet and lowers the head while the pike position is firmly retained. The arms have just started to move inwards.

Fig 99   The drive up through the hips lifts the body. Rotation has started due to the pike position and the head and arms remain in line with the upper body.

Fig 101   The body in flight and fully extended ready for entry.

Diving, Dive Starts and Finishes

Entry *(Fig 102)*

The fingers enter first, followed by the extended body, which, ideally, should be vertical, but an angled entry short of this is acceptable, especially from learners. As the stretched feet and toes enter the water, the dive ends. Skilled divers may go right to the floor of the pool, place their feet down and then push vigorously upwards. Others break their momentum by stretching out the limbs and then reverse their position ready to swim or float to the surface. Some go straight ahead and rise by lifting the arms and head to change direction.

Diving Pre-requisites

1. The learner must be able to open the eyes underwater, to swim underwater and to change direction underwater.
2. The learner must be able to swim several hundred metres or yards, for deep water practices.
3. Diving, like all sports, requires firm self-discipline and class discipline. It is a lively, enjoyable activity where a momentary lapse may have sad consequences.
4. The learner should have the ability to climb out of the pool without using steps, unless the pool design makes it too difficult.
5. The learner should have no difficulty changing from a vertical position in the water to a swimming position as when surfacing.

Teaching Dives

Most children love diving or jumping, but some have very real fears, cured by patience. The following common errors are found at each stage of the plain header:

1. *Stance.* Untidy body position, with feet apart, arms held forward, seat stuck out, belly

Fig 102 *The entry should be vertical, or near vertical, with the body in a straight line. The arms have moved a little out of line.*

pushed forward and, possibly the worst, head held forward.
2. *Take-off.* The arms and/or the head drop forward out of line to cause over-rotation. The hips are not over the feet and the thrust will cause over-rotation. A weak thrust gives the diver little opportunity to achieve height and full extension. Turning the head to one side, or thrusting unequally from the feet, leads to twisting.
3. *Flight.* Excessive piking causes over-rotation and a stiff position with the head held rigid, leads to little or no rotation and a belly-flop. Dropping the head and arms out of line leads to over-rotation.
4. *Entry.* Aiming too far out gives a shallow entry and, conversely, aiming too short, causes the body to go over and the backs of

the legs and seat to smack the water. Crumpling of the body at knee, hip, shoulder, neck and elbow comes from failure to hold the body strongly, but not rigidly, in line.

Coaching divers requires experience, skill and knowledge. The latter may be gained by attending organised Diving Teacher and Coach Courses and by attending seminars.

BACKCRAWL START

Swimming law requires that the feet should be under the water surface, that the swimmer should face the start line and that the hands should be in contact with the end wall of the pool.

Stance *(Figs 103 to 105)*

Swimmers usually wait for the preparatory command of 'take your mark', hanging in a relaxed fashion by the arms. The hands, shoulder width apart, grip the rail, trough or hand-holds on the starting block and the feet may be level and a little apart, or placed one higher than the other. On the order 'take your mark', the arms bend, pulling the body up, and the feet press hard against the wall. It is not permitted to have the feet braced in the trough or against any obtrusion that happens to be present, but very tall swimmers, at the shallow end, have been known to wedge one foot in the angle between the floor and the wall, in order to gain purchase. The head is forward, following the curve of the spine.

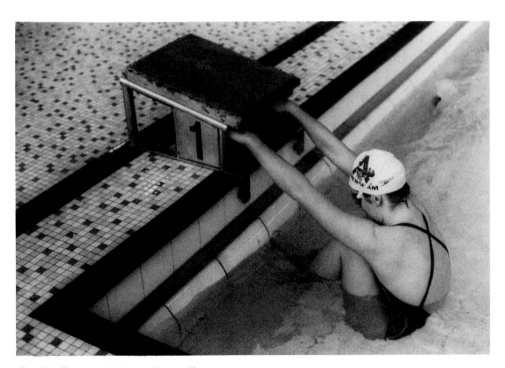

Fig 103 Backcrawl start – waiting position.
The feet may be level and a little apart
or placed one higher than the other.

Fig 104   The backcrawl start position seen
from above the surface.

Fig 105   The backcrawl start position seen
from below the surface. It would be
illegal to lodge the foot against the
fitting on the wall to the left of the
swimmer.

Fig 106 *At the moment of release; note the*
head is well back.

Drive *(Figs 106 to 108)*

A backcrawl start does not have a 'drop' in the same sense as the dive start of the three other strokes, though a technique known as the backcrawl drop start will be described later.

On the starting signal, the swimmer relinquishes the hand grip and should push hard to get the body moving back. Many swimmers just release the hold and swing the arms as the legs are extended. The head is thrown back, which arches the body and raises the hips high in the water. Powerful starters may even have the hips clear the water momentarily, but over-arching leads to an unwanted entry at a big angle and a deep underwater glide.

The arm fling is made in a number of possible ways.

Firstly, the arms are swung straight up and over, a method used by those learning the start and by those who are stiff in the shoulders. If it is too energetically performed, it may add to the difficulties of over-arching, or be its prime cause.

Secondly, the arms are swung in a fan shape round the side of the body, which obviates the risk of over-arching and is used to remedy it.

Thirdly, those with very mobile shoulders have the side fling below the plane of the body.

Fourthly, there are those who sweep the arms up the body, so that the hands pass centrally over the chest and face before straightening into a streamlined position.

A backcrawl drop start has the hands move downwards for the first movement after releasing the grip. The palms move down to smack the water lightly and are then flung back in one of the ways already described. In the split second taken for the hands to move down, the body falls back and is in a better position to have the thrust backwards. The

Fig 107   The head is still back and the hips are
lifting as the body extends.

Fig 108   This swimmer used the drop start
technique. Notice that her arm swing
is developing later.

arms also have a larger radius of action and therefore a larger contribution to make.

Entry

Ideally, the fingertips enter first, an ideal achieved by skilled, strong performers. The body follows the fingers and at this point, the arms and head are leading mainly backwards, but also partly downwards. As more of the body submerges, the arms, head, upper body start to level off, until eventually the whole body is submerged, streamlined and level.

Glide *(Fig 109)*

The depth of glide will match the size of the swimmer and is a little deeper than the depth of the body. The length of the glide will depend on the swimming speed of the individual and it can be extended by kicking underwater. Swimmers should be encouraged to try 'dolphin kick' to see if it improves the starting.

As the body slows to race speed, the head is raised and the first leg kick starts, if not already made, simultaneously with the first arm action. A larger downward component may be present in the arm action to assist the upward movement. The body should break the surface in the natural racing position and the action of the limbs should continue without pause.

Backcrawl Start Pre-requisites

The swimmer must be able to push and glide on the back, underwater.

Fig 109   The body stretches away from the
wall.

Diving, Dive Starts and Finishes

Teaching Backcrawl Start

The sequence for teaching a backcrawl start follows logical steps.

An underwater push and glide on the front must be taught. To it is added a roll to bring the swimmer on to the back, underwater.

A push and glide on the back is made. The swimmer holds the trough and places the feet on the wall at a point which determines the depth of glide. A breath is taken and the swimmer releases the hand grasp, sinks under the water and pushes from the wall, initially gently.

As skill and confidence grow, the strength and length of the underwater glide is increased, until swimmers are asked to swim a half or full width underwater.

Eventually, a backcrawl start is attempted and the swimmer, by trial, finds which of the various arm actions is most satisfactory. From there on regular practice is required.

Coaching Backcrawl Start

All dive starts should be regularly practiced and controlled. Starts are often degraded in training sessions when the swimmer and the coach have one eye on the pace-clock, which leads many coaches to have all swims start with a push from the end. At sessions close to a competition, properly controlled practice conforming to swimming laws is introduced.

A dive start reflects the ability to jump and the latter is strengthened by repeated practice up to a point. Beyond that, extra land training, using body weight exercises, such as tuck jumps, or lifting weights, is required. Many swimmers possess a neat, efficient dive start, but one lacking real power.

RELAY TAKE-OVERS
(Fig 110)

Relay take-overs are dive starts and should be made using the arm wind-up technique. Swimming law requires that the starting signal be given when all competitors are ready and still. A swimmer in a relay is allowed to swing the arms, readying himself for the explosive effort and the arm wind-up technique logically follows. Its main advantage is that it gives a clear view to the swimmer waiting to take over.

The swimmer on the block concentrates on the head of the incoming swimmer. Young competitors can be coached to take up the stance and hold the arms, hands touching, pointing at the head of the swimmer in the water. As the head approaches at steady speed, having been used as an aiming point for the final five or so metres, the arms steadily drop and at a point found by personal experience and with assistance from the coach, the swimmer accelerates the arm movement into an arm swing and then a dive. This action commences before the incoming swimmer has touched and the intent is to have the dive well into its action, but the feet still in contact with the block, or the side, as the touch is made. Should the feet break contact too early, disqualification for the whole team could follow. A long overlap of 'feet and hand' is undesirable and could cost a winning place, or a record. Constant practice, with a final one just prior to the competition, makes relay take-overs razor edged.

FINISHES

Finishes need advice and practice. In races using breaststroke, frontcrawl or backcrawl, a split-second decision is needed as to whether to start another full stroke cycle, or to shorten

Fig 110   *The stance for the wind-up start,
which is the same for a relay take-
over.*

the stroke and reach, meanwhile driving hard with the leg action. Crawl swimmers should be coached to extend the shoulder to lengthen the reach with a sword-like thrust. Backcrawlers must not roll onto the front until after the touch.

Butterfly swimmers must recover the arms over the water and, if the finish is close, must decide whether to take another stroke and touch with the hands wide, as part of the recovery action, or hold the arms extended in front and kick vigorously for the wall, keeping the head down for streamlining to the end, where medals may be won or lost. Though practice is of great help, competition experience cannot be bought. The incoming swimmer in a relay race must finish well to give the outgoing partner and the team every chance.

Completing a Race

To complete a race, a breaststroke swimmer must touch the wall above, below, or on the water level, with the hands at the same level and at the same time.

To complete a race, a butterfly swimmer must touch as does a breaststroke swimmer.

To complete a race, a frontcrawl swimmer must touch, with any part of the body. Obviously a hand touch is preferable.

To complete a race, a backcrawl swimmer must touch with the leading hand, or arm, or the leading part of the body. Obviously a hand touch is preferable.

The word 'touch' is used in swimming laws and has been used above. It gives an impression which contrasts with the rapid, strong, stabbing movement required in competition.

RELAY SWIMMING

Specific competitions require that the order of swimming of the team be declared at a given time before the event. Some do not and the coach might decide on a tactical switch of order during the event. A reliable starter avoids chance of disqualification for the whole team.

Some coaches place the swimmers in speed order, slowest first. If the speed differences are slight, then consideration may be given to other factors, such as starting and take-over skills, breathing sides on the final leg in order to watch the closest opposition and temperament for a fighting finish. Should the speed differences be wide, it is often a waste to have the fastest swimmer go last. A tactical switch could be prepared or the fastest swimmers go before the slowest, to give a lead that might be held. The pressure is on the slow last swimmer to respond.

Records can be made by the first swimmer and it might be necessary to ask the co-operation of race officials in advance.

7 Turns

INTRODUCTION
(Figs 111 to 114)

Although the turns regularly used in the four recognised strokes may look very different to the casual observer, they have more in common than appears.

There has already been discussion of the three ranges of movement at a joint, the inner, middle and outer ranges. In a turn, as in a start, the swimmer places the body with the knees and hip in the middle range, the strong one, and skilled, powerful performers position the body at the edge of the middle and outer range, to take advantage of the strength and speed of the movement. A gymnast, in performing a vault, runs to jump first from the feet and then from the hands. In most turns, a swimmer races to the wall and jumps off the hands and then off the feet. Because a swimming turn is slowed down by the resistance of the water, its explosive, gymnastic quality is frequently unnoticed.

Swimming law imposes conditions for turns, to be detailed later, but when the three factors below are combined, the strong similarities of the turns become evident.

1. Laws of the turns and also the strokes.
2. Range of activity used.
3. Explosive, gymnastic skill.

FRONTCRAWL TURN
(Figs 115 to 122)

Frontcrawl turns require a touch with any part of the body, and all competitors use a racing tumble turn. It starts well away from the wall and, as it is executed, the swimmer's body is still moving rapidly towards the wall. The head and shoulders are pushed down as the arms are pulled to the side of the body, often one pulling across to aid the twisting movement which turns the body onto the side. The legs give a dolphin type flip to aid the impetus towards the wall before lifting from the water and whipping over at speed to plunge back into the water. The swimmer sculls with one hand to aid the rotation, and at this point the arms have moved up above the head, but with the elbows well flexed. The swimmer is on the side, with the whole body in the water, deeper than the normal position, due to the overwater movement of the legs. The feet are clear of the wall in a well performed turn.

From this position, the hips and knees are strongly extended to bounce the feet on the wall in an action similar to that used in a double footed jump. Streamlining is achieved by stretching the arms, hands side by side, or preferably one on top of the other, and finally the feet aid the powerful push with their extension as in a plain header. The swimmer turns onto the front and as the body slows to racing speed, the first leg and arm actions, coupled with natural buoyancy and a lift of the head, bring the swimmer to the surface in a racing position, at race speed and with the arms and legs already in their racing action.

Fig 111   A gymnast jumps first off the feet . . .

Fig 112   . . . and then off the hands.

Fig 113   A swimmer turns by jumping first off
                the hand (or hands) . . .

Fig 114. . . and then off the feet.

Frontcrawl Turn Sequence

Fig 115 The approach is made without slackening speed. One arm stops at the end of its push, and the head and shoulders are dropped to lead into a front somersault as the other hand ends its action.

Fig 117 Both arms are levering powerfully to aid rapid rotation.

Fig 116 Many swimmers add a dolphin flip of the legs at this point.

Fig 118 The swirl continues as the feet near the wall and the body opens out.

Fig 119 *Swirl, body twist and body extensions prepare for the powerful 'jump' off the feet.*

Fig 121 *The streamlined push-off is made with the body on its side. Notice better streamlining aided by placing one hand on top of the other, bringing the arms tight against the head.*

Fig 120 *The feet hit the wall in perfect timing for a powerful streamlined push-off. Notice the 'outer range' position achieved.*

Fig 122 *The body rolls onto its front as the hands and feet start the stroke which will drive the swimmer forwards and upwards, ready to continue the action at speed and without pause.*

BACKCRAWL TURN
(Figs 123 to 132)

After the touch with the leading part of the body, arm or hand, the swimmer is permitted to turn off the back as required while swimming. The touch is made with an extended arm, palm flat against the wall, fingers pointing down. An important consideration is the depth of the touch, as eventually the feet are placed close to that point, which will govern the depth of the underwater push and glide. The head and shoulders are pressed back and the legs, having kicked hard all the way in, begin to bend at the knee.

From this point, for most competitive swimmers, there are two actions to be seen. One has the hand remaining on the wall and the other, stronger action, has a powerful push from the hand, the jump off the hands which denotes gymnastic power. The weaker action will be described first.

Using the hand and arm as a support, the lower legs and part of the upper leg are lifted from the water. The free arm and hand scull across the body to turn it partly on the side and to rotate it. As the legs are raised, the trunk sinks lower in the water. The arm pressing its hand to the wall is sometimes long and straight and sometimes has flexion at the elbow. If flexion is present, the arm straightens while the hips twist to bring the legs and feet sideways into the water. The touching hand moves away from the wall as the feet are planted. Should there be no flexion, or very little, the hand is lifted from the wall, adding no strength to the rotation.

The body is now on its side, feet against the wall, knees and hips well flexed in middle range, with the arms moving up the body. The legs and hips straighten at the same time as the arms extend to a streamlined position, the feet adding the final push from the wall. This part of the turn has no jump from the hand and little or no jump or bounce from the feet. It is a weak action.

A stronger action is used in the other turn, in which there is a definite, powerful push, or jump from the hand, which sets the body rotating earlier and more rapidly, aided by the free hand. Because the hand has pushed strongly, the body is further away from the wall and there is more room for it to position itself where the hips and knees can thrust the feet against the wall for the desired jump, or bounce.

The streamlining is the same in both versions. Usually the performer pushes off on the side, though a rotation action will soon put the body on the back, as required by swimming law, before any stroke is made. Surfacing is performed so that the position is one ready for immediate racing and has been generalised and described earlier.

The speed reached by national and world class backcrawl swimmers is such that their turns are shallower than those described above and show well the powerful jumping action of hand and feet. Slow motion film reveals that the face is high in the water and the hips down, so that the name of the turn, 'the bucket turn', is very descriptive. It is performed as if the swimmer has the hips in a bucket and pivots round at speed in that position.

Front and Backcrawl Turn Pre-requisites

1. The ability to push and glide on the front, on the side and on the back.
2. The ability to somersault forward and backward from a standing position in shoulder-depth water.

Keen-eyed teachers will see that the somersaults are often achieved by help from the arms which are stretched out sideways and sculling, to aid the turning motion. A similar sculling action is used in crawl turns. While checking the turns in a practice session, it takes only a moment to see if the arms are out sideways, as with those just learning, or close to the body, like the experts.

Teaching Frontcrawl Turn

Exercises

1. Well away from the wall, swim head up dog-paddle to a somersault. Then stand up.
2. Swim head down dog-paddle to a somersault. Stand up.
3. Swim frontcrawl to a somersault. Stand up.
4. Dog-paddle with the head up from a few metres out to somersault to the wall. Plant the feet on the wall. Stop and stand up. The object of the practice is to help the swimmer measure the distance from the wall needed to make the turn.
5. Dog-paddle head down to somersault and plant the feet on the wall. Stop and stand up.
6. Combine the dog-paddle approach, the somersault and the known push and glide by swimming dog-paddle head up, somersaulting and adding a push and glide.
7. As confidence and skill grow, approach the wall using head down dog-paddle and, finally, a gentle frontcrawl.

Demonstrations given frequently by skilled swimmers will aid in building a skilled, polished turn.

Teaching Backcrawl Turn

Exercises

1. Swim back-paddle with one arm sculling, the other extended beyond the head.
2. Swim as above to the wall, to feel the hand

touch firmly. Stop and stand up. The practice is designed to remove the fear of swimming head first towards the wall.
3. Swim backcrawl towards the wall and for the last few strokes, use one arm for swimming, while holding the other extended for the touch.
4. Stand with the back to the wall, shoulders under, one arm extended backward to grasp the rail, or trough, or to be held firmly against the wall. The position gives the swimmer the exact position of the wall, at arm's length, even though it cannot be seen.
5. On a signal, jump while pushing with the hand to twist the body to face the wall, at the same time bending the knees and hips. The feet are planted on the wall and the body falls back in a position ready for the push and glide, as previously taught from a roll back and described in the backcrawl start.
6. Swim back-paddle, with one hand sculling, the other extended, to touch the wall and then turn as performed in the previous practice.
7. Swim one arm backcrawl to perform the turn and finally swim gentle full stroke into a turn.

As confidence and skill are acquired, the speed and strength of the turn will grow.

BREASTSTROKE TURN
(Figs 133 to 141)

At a turn, the swimmer is currently required to touch simultaneously with both hands, but they may be at different levels.

The approach to the wall is at speed, with no hesitation, as in all turns. Some swimmers touch with the hands close together, others with them shoulder width or more apart, and the hand which is on the side to which the turn will be made is the lower, should the hands be

Backcrawl Turn Sequence

Fig 123   The leg kick drives the body to a
well-timed touch, fingers down.

Fig 124   The head is dropping back. The
non-touching arm and hand
complete the action.

Fig 125   The legs are up and over, while the
body spins from the push of the
touching hand and the sculling of the
non-touching hand.

Fig 126   The touching hand has pushed free
of the wall.

Fig 127   The non-touching hand can just be
seen. The knees and hips are in mid-
range position.

Fig 130   The arms are stretching to a
streamlined position as the feet
prepare to jump off the wall.

Fig 128   The body unrolls to flatten the back
as the leg drive starts and the arms
extend for streamlining. This turn is
completed with toes pointing
straight up.

Fig 131   All is ready for a powerful thrust.

Fig 129   The legs are accelerating towards
the wall.

Fig 132   The body stretches away from the
wall.

at different levels. Swimmers must keep the shoulders square and level up to the touch.

Swimming speed brings the head close to the wall as the elbows flex in order to provide power for the push or jump off the hands. The shoulder to the turning side drops and the hand is taken from the wall, by bending the elbow and tucking it to the side underwater.

Fig 135   The feet are ready to jump as the head enters the water, soon to be followed by the pushing arm.

Fig 133   The touch can be made with the hands at different levels, but the body must be square and level until the touch is made.

Fig 136   Following a glide, the arms make a pull and push similar to a butterfly arm action. Note the high elbow position.

Fig 134   The body swings like a pendulum and the ankles cross as one arm pushes powerfully away from the wall.

Fig 137   The hands pass close under the body.

Fig 138   Another glide follows the arm action
and the head is held down to keep
sufficient depth for the ensuing leg
action.

Fig 140   Everything is ready for the leg kick
which drives the body to the surface.

Fig 139   Arms and legs recover together and
the head is raised in preparation for
surfacing. Note the hands are palm
down, which tucks the elbows in.

Fig 141   The legs have kicked and the head
has broken surface, at which point
the arms are ready to continue the
stroke cycle.

The body is spinning round and the hips and knees are flexing and swinging pendulum fashion towards the wall.

Some swimmers turn the head with the shoulder in the direction of the turn. Others keep the face to the wall and snatch a quick breath.

Swimmers who are strong in the arm and shoulder push powerfully off the wall, which gives added rotation, momentum and space to the turn. Space is important, because a truly explosive effort has the swimmer momentarily still turning without contact on the wall. As the body assumes a more horizontal position, the legs have opportunity for the powerful jump and rebound action which provides the best push. If the hand is kept in contact with the wall, a slower action all round eventuates, because the arm straightens slowly. The difference between an explosive push and a slow straightening of the arm is obvious to an observer, but the weakest arm push action derives from a touch made with long straight arms, of which the one retained on the wall stays straight.

After the pendulum swing is completed, the swimmer is on the side, feet and hips flexed, or partly on the side and the front. Usually the feet plant on the wall side by side horizontally. The pushing arm is flexed and circled over the head, so that the eyes are looking under it, or it may be behind the head. Both hands touch, side by side, or one on top of the other and the whole body extends, in a push ending with the foot extension and a position streamlined from fingers to toes. A roll is made to bring the body face down before any strokes are made, in compliance with swimming law.

The push and glide in a breaststroke turn is made with the feet positioned deeper on the wall than in the other turns, in order that the swimmer may take advantage of the permitted underwater stroke, which is identical with that following a start and has already been described. Eventually the swimmer surfaces and obeys swimming law by commencing the stroke after part of the head has risen clear of the water.

Breaststroke Turn Pre-requisites

1. The ability to swim breaststroke underwater.
2. The ability to push and glide on the front and on the side.

Teaching Breaststroke Turn

Exercises

1. Swim in hard from a few metres out, to gain experience of judging the touch.
2. Stand at arm's length facing the wall, shoulders under, both hands grasping the rail or trough. On command, jump, twist with one hand holding the trough, to turn and plant the feet. Sink below the surface and then push and glide. Float to the surface and stop.

Combine the two exercises above. When the turn is sufficiently mastered, add the underwater strokes, stretching out their rhythm thus:

Push and glide – hold the glide.
Arm pull – hold the glide.

Arms and legs recover together, and the leg kick combines with the lift of the head and natural buoyancy to bring the swimmer to the surface.

Coaching Breaststroke Turn

Checkpoints

1. Look to see if a breath is snatched on the turn, slowing it down.
2. The head should come in close to the wall if the arms are really bending, ready for a strong push, or jump action.
3. There is sometimes a lift of the body which causes it to sink in order to get the feet low on the wall. Normally it is a natural action. If it is missing, the feet could be too high, giving a downward push to get the depth required for the underwater stroke, or the underwater position could be too shallow. A few swimmers exaggerate the body lift and consequently sink too deep, needing then an upward thrust from the wall to compensate.
4. In the underwater action, coach your swimmers in crossing the hands underwater to see if it helps.

Breaststroke tumble turns, touching with the backs of the hands, fingers down and sliding them down the wall and following them with the head and body, which then twists to bring the feet on the wall, provides variety and a fun activity.

Slow turns derive more from lack of strength than lack of skill. A training programme in the gymnasium, using weights, or body weight, provides an answer.

BUTTERFLY TURN
(Figs 142 to 147)

The butterfly turn has similarities, at certain stages, to the breaststroke turn.

During the approach to the wall, the swimmer's head rises and falls, so that the clear view afforded by breaststroke is absent. Much practice is required to gain the experience for accurate judgement of whether to make another stroke or not, or to drive in to the touch with the legs only. Swimming law requires the limb movements to be simultaneous and symmetrical, so whether at above or below the surface, the touch must be made accordingly, at the width favoured by the individual.

If the head is down in the water at the moment of the touch, it is raised and the momentum of the swim brings the head close to the wall, the elbows flexing to accommodate this. Butterfly swimmers are more likely to snatch a breath at the turn than breaststrokers and the face is turned to the wall accordingly, as the arms and shoulders follow the same pattern described in a breaststroke turn. Butterfly swimmers need upper body strength for success in the stroke and consequently have a strong arm thrust.

A shallow push off the wall meets the needs of the stroke and the feet are placed on the wall at a depth suitable for the swimmer's build, side by side and horizontal, usually. The powerful stretch of the body, legs and feet is as described in the breaststroke turn, bringing the swimmer away from the wall on the side.

Rotation onto the front is necessary before any strokes are made, to comply with swimming law.

For first class butterfly swimmers, there is a short, shallow, streamlined glide, before the head is lifted, the legs kick and hands start to press down and back. These movements, plus natural buoyancy, bring the swimmer to the surface in a racing position at race speed, with no check in the arm action, which is timed to make recovery as the body breaks the water level. Slower swimmers may make two or more leg kicks to extend the glide after slowing down to racing speed. It is sound practice to hold the breath for the first stroke or two in order to ensure a correct body position, because raising the head immediately on surfacing, would compound any slight deviations.

Butterfly Turn Pre-requisites

1. The ability to push and glide, on the front and on the side.
2. The ability to swim dolphin leg kick underwater, at a controlled depth, with arms streamlined in front of the head.

Teaching Butterfly Turn

Teaching sequences which parallel those already described for breaststroke are developed. The most important practices initially relate to accurate judgement of the approach and the touch.

Coaching Butterfly Turn

Checkpoints

1. Watch to see when the swimmer takes breath on the approach to and after the turn.
2. Ensure that the swimmer is aware of

markings on the floor and the end wall of the pool which assist in judging the approach.

3. Similarly, ensure that the swimmer is aware of any changes in colour of the lane ropes which signal the distance to the wall.

4. In the warm-up, practise turns at full speed to assess the grip obtainable on the wall.

5. In older pools, with rails, troughs and over-hanging edges, ask officials which is the correct turning and finishing place.

6. Butterfly somersault turns, touching with the backs of the hands, add variety and fun to a session.

Fig 144 *While the pendulum swing continues, the swimmer has opportunity for a quick breath. Most swimmers cross the ankles at this stage, further shortening the lever for increased speed of movement.*

Fig 142 *The approach is made without loss of speed and is timed to comply with swimming law.*

Fig 145 *The pendulum action is completed as the feet plant on the wall. Above water, the head and arm are swinging downwards. Notice that the outer range position seen in the frontcrawl turn cannot be achieved because swimming law requires the two-handed touch which brings the body close to the wall.*

Fig 143 *After a legal touch has been made, one hand slips off the wall and aids the pendulum swing of the body and its rotation. Notice the elbow bend of the arm on the wall, which will give a strong 'jump' off the hand.*

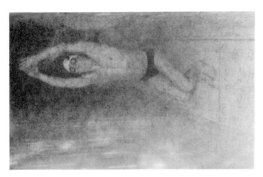

Fig 146 The 'bounce' off the wall is under
way, with the body adopting a
streamlined position to take full
advantage of the thrust.

Fig 147 The push can be made with the body
on its side, but before any stroke
commences, the position required by
swimming law must be taken. The
initial kick or kicks combine with the
first arm action to thrust the body
forward and upward in a swimming
position, ready to continue the stroke
without pause.

MEDLEY TURNS

Butterfly to Backcrawl

The touch must be as described for a butterfly
turn. From a 'head-in close' position, both
arms are vigorously extended as the body
sinks below the surface, falling back and flexing at the hip and knee, ready for a powerful
push after the feet are planted on the wall.

Alternatively, following the touch, one arm
and shoulder drop, as described in a butterfly
turn, so that the subsequent thrust is with the
body on the side. The swimmer takes up a
position on the back before commencing
backcrawl.

Backcrawl to Breaststroke
(Figs 148 to 154)

Directly the leading hand has touched, the
head and shoulders sink and the legs rise in a
back-roll movement. The touching arm
pushes hard to aid rotation and the free hand
sculls for the same reason, until the feet are
planted on the wall, toes pointing somewhere
between the horizontal and vertically downward. After the normal powerful push, the
body must be on the front before any stroke is
taken, underwater or at the surface.

Another version of this turn, more often
seen in the 400 metres Individual Medley, is
for the touch to comply with backstroke law,
following which the body turns on the side,
with the arm shortening and the body gather-
ing ready for the feet to be planted. It is a head
up turn which allows a breath to be snatched.
The feet are placed at the depth for the push
and glide to be followed by the underwater
stroke sequence and surfacing already described.

Turns

Fig 148 *The approach and touch must comply with swimming law.*

Fig 150 *The touching arm must stay long to give space into which the legs will drop, after the back somersault.*

Fig 149 *The touching arm stays long as the head drops to lead the body into a back somersault.*

Fig 151 *At this point the body is free of the wall and rotating more rapidly due to shortening of the lever.*

Fig 152 *The feet are ready for a vigorous push and the arms and body are moving into position for a push-off at the depth and angle appropriate to the individual swimmer.*

Fig 153 *A streamlined position is held at a depth which will accommodate the underwater stroke.*

Fig 154 *The transition to racing stroke is exactly as in a breaststroke start or turn.*

Breaststroke to Frontcrawl

Swimming laws already described apply to the touch, and the turn has all the appearance of being a normal breaststroke turn, except that it is shallower and the swimming speed for frontcrawl is reached quickly.

Coaching Medley Turns

Checkpoints

1. Think of medley turns as fast to slow, slow to fast and so on. The swimmer must be physically and mentally ready for the change in rhythm after each turn.

2. Medley turns in the 200m are faster than 400m medley turns. Somersaults are seen more.

3. Practise across the width, so that speed is high and fatigue is low.

4. All swimmers must learn the medley sequences and the various turns available, at least for use in training and preferably for competition.

8 Hygiene, Health and Safety

HYGIENE

Visitors to the local pool should be clean, free of open or running sores, have a clean nose and feet without infections.

A call to the toilet should be made before a shower, and after the swim another quick shower should be taken. Clean towels are essential, and small children should be taught to spread the toes with one hand and use a portion of dry towel to dry thoroughly between the toes. Swimming costumes require regular laundering, just like the rest of a wardrobe.

Those possessors of long hair should wear a bathing cap in order to keep the wet locks from the eyes and also for the benefit of the pool staff responsible for cleaning, and other bathers.

Ear troubles are best treated by your doctor, who should be consulted before a swimmer takes up hard, competitive training. Also, after prolonged illness, medical advice should be sought before taking even limited exercise.

HEALTH

Younger and older children, parents and grandparents can all enjoy a visit to the pool, for swimming is generally free of injury risks. When the human body is in water, it becomes weightless, which is an aid to those who are weak. Further, certain changes occur in the shape and capacity of the heart, making swimming of extra value to those whose heart might not be at its best.

Fitness *(Figs 156 to 160)*

Those trying to get back a measure of fitness, who do not relish jogging, but opt for swimming, should build the fitness progressively. Do not measure how far you swim, but first measure for how long you are able to keep moving and do not be ashamed to use a float. It might for the first week or so be just minutes,

Fig 155   A routine hygiene check is under way.

but perseverance will build it up rapidly, and when you are able to swim easily and steadily, start counting how many lengths you achieve in a given time. There is usually either a large pace clock, or a public clock which will be accurate enough.

Distance is the important factor, not speed, because a few lengths as fast as possible will leave the swimmer depleted. It is the basis of aerobic exercise, of which much is spoken and written.

The human body has two main fuels, fat and carbohydrate. Any excess food eaten is converted to fat and stored, a fact which gives rise to the grim warning, 'a moment on the lips, a lifetime on the hips'. Carbohydrate, which is sugar, or starch from bread and potatoes, is available as glycogen to power the muscles. First it is converted to pyruvic acid, which creates the chemicals that combine with the oxygen breathed in, to enable the muscles to work. There is no time limit, virtually, and this aerobic chemical action is the basis of most of everyday activity and of most physical exercise.

If the exercise rate is pushed too high, the body is unable to supply sufficient oxygen and automatically it switches to an alternative system, which works in the absence of oxygen and is called anaerobic.

Every five units of pyruvic acid organise themselves so that four give what oxygen they have to the fifth. The four are out of action at once and, in giving away the precious oxygen,

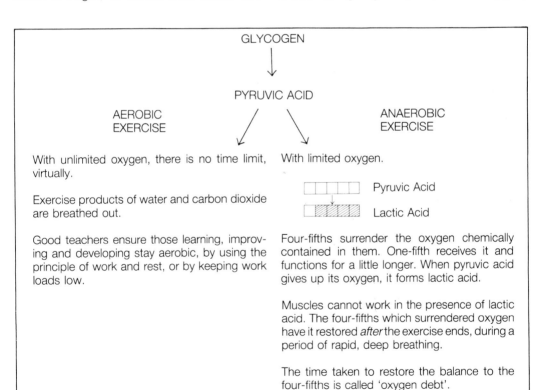

Fig 156   Energy systems.

they have changed to lactic acid. The fifth unit works until it has consumed what oxygen it has and then all activity ceases. Muscles are unable to work in the presence of lactic acid.

Sometimes the lactic acid will be manufactured in one group of muscles, as when performing press-ups. Eventually the blood supply is unable to wash the lactic acid away and the arm muscles cease the activity. Sometimes, if the exercise involves the whole body, as in swimming frontcrawl very quickly, lactic acid spills over everywhere in the body and the swimmer stops. There are people with high lactic acid tolerance, but most people give in earlier.

After the exercise has ended, the swimmer continues to breathe heavily, because the four-fifths of the pyruvic acid, which surrendered the oxygen, have it returned. It explains what is meant by 'oxygen debt', which is the period of time taken to rebuild the pyruvic acid and hence, the glycogen.

Training

Swimming training, for those who wish to retain some level of fitness, or those who aim to be a first class swimmer, involves training the aerobic system before the anaerobic system. It should follow the path:

1. Skill.
2. Aerobic fitness.
3. Anaerobic fitness.

Fig 157   Flexibility of the shoulders is essential for swimming. Work in the gymnasium improves it.

Fig 158   Strong arms are needed for strokes and turns. The exercise is a bench press.

Most people are concerned with gaining some or all of the skills of swimming. Fewer are interested in acquiring aerobic fitness and exercise themselves by continuous movement over longer periods. A small few go on to train the anaerobic power of the body.

Skill development might take a few hours weekly. Aerobic power might take up to eight or ten hours weekly. Full anaerobic power, combined with aerobic power will take over twenty hours weekly, with a competent coach to help.

The hours quoted are variable and depend on genetic characteristics, as well as personal psychology. There are those who enjoy crossing the threshold from aerobic to anaerobic exercise and holding on.

At whichever level an individual chooses to exercise, it is best to start young, before puberty, and create a body which will last handsomely a lifetime. Take to heart the cautionary remarks elsewhere on letting swimmers mature after puberty. Do not expect children to perform like adults.

SAFETY

Diving, along with jumping, is the source of the more serious injuries at a swimming pool. The teacher and coach, or the parent, have responsibilities to make certain that the diving area is roped off, if possible, and kept clear. Divers, after surfacing, should never return to

Fig 159 Strength is gained rapidly, even with light weights. This exercise will improve the butterfly push phase.

Fig 160 Total body strength is an asset and working at high pulls is worthwhile.

the diving area and discipline must be maintained at all times.

A golden rule for teachers of learners and improvers is that no child dives in unless instructed to do so. A similar rule for jumping should be enforced, if needed.

Pool 'geography', with permitted areas and forbidden areas, must be explained on the first visit to a particular pool. Children learn quickly where to wait and where to enter the water and constant reminders do not come amiss.

Diving requires a depth of 8ft 6in (2.6m) for a good, safe performance of the English header, but experience has evolved the following rule of thumb for the depth of water when teaching elementary stages:

1. The sitting dive – shoulder depth of the performer.
2. Kneeling dive – height of the performer.
3. Lunge dive and above – reach height of the performer.

Hypothermia

Hypothermia, if written as hyp–O–thermia, is a reminder of the not quite total absence of heat, but of its loss. Most people are familiar with temperatures taken at the mouth, and less aware of the importance of core temperature in the centre of the body, around the vital organs. Survival studies in arduous conditions are revealing realistic ways of reducing heat loss. The only safe way is to wear a life-jacket of approved design, whether a good swimmer or not and, in truly adverse conditions of water temperature and wind, to wear survival clothing of an approved type, such as a wetsuit.

In less severe conditions, thin people, especially children, are liable to lose a couple of degrees centigrade in an ordinary swimming lesson. Think of those white skins, blue lips and fingernails and spasms of shivering that are seen. Such people, especially children,

must be sent to dress at once. Similar loss of heat occurs on the beach and wise parents and teachers will look for it.

Those taking part in water sports should be properly equipped, but all should observe the following rules, some of which apply at the local pool and in the private one at home:

1. Never swim alone.
2. Never swim when the danger flags are flying.
3. Find the areas designated as safer for swimming.
4. In a small boat accident, off-shore, stay with the wreckage. Many non-swimmers have been saved because of clinging to wreckage.
5. Frozen water is attractive but deadly.
6. If alone, retain clothing and huddle to conserve heat.
7. If in a group, huddle to share heat and to reduce its loss.

Life-saving

Training and constant practice are needed, but most people lack the time or temperament for it. Commonsense makes a helpful substitute and some rules are listed below:

1. If you are a non-swimmer or a weak swimmer, do not enter the water to help. Summon aid if it is close by.
2. Any floating object, such as a play-ball, makes a life-float.
3. Reach as far as possible towards the person in the water and extend the reach with poles, cardigans, ropes and anything that will cover the gap.

Prevention is better than cure and everywhere people are in or on water in numbers, safety aids should be easily accessible. A list includes first-aid box, telephone, light but strong poles, ropes, oxygen mask, stretcher

Fig 161   A solo huddle position hugging a
float.

and blankets and, not least, trained life-savers. It is the speed of rescue that counts, because shock may be as damaging as hypothermia or partial drowning.

Pool authorities have a responsibility to ensure that water depths are clearly marked and to remember the poor sight of some of the bathers. Teachers have a heavy responsibility to see that young swimmers are aware of the perils of swimming to the limit of ability. A width of deep water could be lethal to a one-width swimmer.

SPECIAL CLASSES

Adult Learners

Many authorities provide, through the schools, an excellent swimming development programme as part of physical and social education. Adult requirements are met in the evenings with provision of a knowledgeable teacher and water space and time away from public hours.

Inquiry at the local pool will provide information, as it will of club activities covering swimming, diving, synchro-swimming, life-saving, water polo and recreational needs.

Baby and Parent Classes

An interesting development is the growth of special provision for babies, more usually with the mother, to enjoy water activities. Provision is made for the baby's needs, from nappy changing facilities, to a quiet atmosphere and smooth water. Ask at the local pool, but inquire about the qualifications of the teacher. The great majority of the classes create an

Fig 162   The boy has hearing loss and the
teacher is ensuring, by eye to eye
contact and touch, that he knows
exactly what to do.

easy, relaxed, enjoyable and instructive
atmosphere, providing graded development,
which is as it should be.

Handicapped Classes

It is heartening to record that authorities are
providing more time and space for the less
fortunate in our society. Graded classes, leading to certification of teachers, are available
and inquiries should be made at the local pool,
or local club.

Summary

The four recognised strokes used in competition have been described and some mention has been made of others.

Imagine now a swimmer using breaststroke, who rolls to one side and changes to side stroke, with the face of the water. To gain speed, an overwater recovery is taken by the upper arm and, to increase speed again, the body is rolled from side to side and the head turned from side to side, as each arm recovers through the air. The stroke has become the trudgeon, with frontcrawl arms and breaststroke legs.

The face is lowered into the water and the legs, with toes pointed, start to kick up and down as the stroke is translated into frontcrawl. When the arms begin to move synchronously, and also the legs, it has switched to butterfly. A reversion is made to breaststroke leg action and the swimmer rolls completely onto the back, swimming Old English backstroke, with its double arm action. A rest is given to the arms and the swimmer relies on legs only in the life-saving leg kick, but when the arms begin again, it is with an alternating windmill action, with which the legs co-ordinate in an up and down alternating kick. The stroke is backcrawl.

Again the swimmer rolls onto the side, so that the legs have a wide scissor kick with pointed toes and the lower arm must recover in the water. It is side stroke again. A roll onto the front, coupled with simultaneous kicks from legs having dorsiflexed feet and arms working totally underwater, takes the cycle to where it started, with breaststroke.

Four of the strokes in the whole cycle are recognised, but all other positions and combinations are recognisable where people swim in the waters of the earth.

Glossary

Action   In swimming, a movement of the limbs. For every action there is an equal and opposite reaction.

Aerobic   Loosely, exercise for which there is sufficient oxygen. It relates to endurance.

Anaerobic   Loosely, exercise for which the oxygen supply is insufficient. It relates to sprinting.

Anatomy   Study of the materials which form the parts of the body and how the parts fit together.

Back-paddle   Swimming on the back, with a crawl-type leg kick and with the hands making propeller movements close by the hips. Sometimes loosely called 'sculling'.

Ballistic   In swimming, a rapid flinging action of the arms in recovery.

Bent arm   The most skilled and effective way of using the arms in all swimming strokes.

Breathing   Moving air into and out of the lungs.
  aquatic ; skilled control of breathing while the head is intermittantly partly or completely submerged.
  bilateral ; in frontcrawl, breathing to alternate sides every 1½ stroke cycles.
  early ; breathing before the opportune moment.
  late ; breathing after the opportune moment.
  trickle ; Slow, unhurried breathing.

Catch point   Where the hands begin to exert pressure on the water. Ideally, it should be as early as possible.

Catch up   A style of swimming crawl strokes where one arm waits just before catch point for the other to join it. Used also as training skill. Sometimes referred to as 'sliding', or 'overlap'.

Co-ordination   The interlinking of arm and leg movements with breathing which produces swimming.

Dog-paddle   Swimming on the front using an alternating crawl leg kick and an alternating arm action, with an underwater recovery.

Dorsi-flexed   Turning the feet up, as in breaststroke.

Drill   A practice used in a swimming session, usually by a coach.

Elbow leading   An arm action which has the forearm slipping inefficiently backwards through the water. It is the opposite of high elbow.

Endurance   The ability to keep on exerting force against a resistance. Cardio-vascular endurance relates to the whole body. Local muscle endurance relates to specific limbs or muscle groups.

Exhalation   Breathing out and the opposite of inhalation.

Extension The opening of a joint, and the opposite of flexion.

Flexibility That quality which permits large movements at a joint. Sometimes called mobility.

Glycogen Basic energy source stored in muscles and liver.

High elbow (1) A type of arm recovery in frontcrawl, with the arm close to the head and the elbow well flexed. (2) A technique used in all strokes where the arms are well flexed and the forearm pointing downwards when level with the shoulders.

Hypothermia Loss of heat at the vital core of the body.

Inertia Resistance to movement.

Lactic acid By-product of anaerobic exercise. Muscles cannot contract in its presence.

Lever A rigid structure exerting force across a point of balance. The limbs are used as levers.

Multi-stroke Beginners attempt several ways of swimming, then develop that which suits them, while still learning all.

Oxygen debt The amount of oxygen needed to return the body to normal, following anaerobic exercise.

Physiology Study of how the body functions.

Pitch The angle at which the hands and feet move through the water. Related to thrust via Bernoulli principles.

Plantar-flexion Pointing of the feet and toes as in crawl-type kicking.

Prone The 'on' in the middle means the body is on its face.

Pull-push Description of the long movement of the arms possible. The pull ends at shoulder level.

Pyruvic acid One stage in the long chemical chain producing energy.

Recovery Movements which return the limb to the position from which they started.

Respiration The whole complicated action of moving oxygen into the lungs and thence to the tissues and of removing carbon dioxide.

Sculling Propulsion obtained by small hand movements accompanied by changes of pitch.

Straight arm Loose term for style using little elbow flexion and consequently little or no pitch change of hands.

Strength Ability to exert force against a resistance. *See Endurance.*

Supine On the back. Remember it by removing the letter 'u', to form 'spine'.

Training Term used to describe wide range of organised preparation for physical performance.

Warm-down After demanding exercise, further similar, but gentler movement speeds recovery.

Warm-up Initial exercise to prepare the

Glossary

body physiologically and psychologically for strenuous activity.

Wedge kick Inefficient breaststroke leg action, which presents the sole of the foot to the water and offers high resistance with low limb acceleration.

Whip kick Efficient breaststroke leg action, which presents large inner area of foot to the water and offers low resistance with high limb acceleration.

Index

Index

Index

Other Titles in The Skills of the Game Series

◆   Also available in paperback

Further details of titles available or in preparation can be obtained from the publishers.